INSIDE WORDS

JANET ALLEN

INSIDE WORDS

TOOLS FOR TEACHING ACADEMIC VOCABULARY GRADES 4–12

STENHOUSE PUBLISHERS
PORTLAND, MAINE

KH

Stenhouse Publishers
www.stenhouse.com

Credit
Page 5: "What Do We Know from Research?" Previously published in "The Art of Effective Vocabulary Instruction," by Janet Allen. In *Adolescent Literacy*, edited by Kylene Beers, Robert E. Probst, and Linda Rief. Copyright © 2007. Used by permission of the publisher, Heinemann.

Library of Congress Cataloging-in-Publication Data
Allen, Janet, 1950–
    Inside words : tools for teaching academic vocabulary, grades 4–12 / Janet Allen.
        p. cm.
    Includes bibliographical references.
    ISBN 978-1-57110-399-4 (alk. paper)
    1. Vocabulary—Study and teaching. 2. Language arts. I. Title.
    LB1574.5.A43 2007
    418'.0071—dc22   2007024330

Cover, interior design, and typeset by Martha Drury
Manufactured in the United States of America on acid-free, recycled paper
13 12 11 10 09 08   9 8 7 6 5 4 3

9/9/09

CONTENTS

Instructional Strategies and the Tools
    That Support Them   *vii*
Acknowledgments   *xi*
Introduction   *1*

CONCEPT CIRCLES   13
CONCEPT LADDER   19
CONCEPTS AND VOCABULARY: CATEGORIES AND LABELS   25
CONTEXTUAL REDEFINITION   31
DICTOGLOS   35
FOCUSED CLOZE   39
FRAYER MODEL   43
FREQUENT CONTACT   49

"I'M THINKING OF A WORD . . ."   55

I SPY: A WORD SCAVENGER HUNT   59

LEAD   63

LIST-GROUP-LABEL   69

POSSIBLE QUESTIONS   75

POSSIBLE SENTENCES   81

PREVIEWING CONTENT VOCABULARY   87

SEMANTIC FEATURE ANALYSIS   91

SEMANTIC MAPPING   97

SURVIVAL OF THE FITTEST   101

THINK-PAIR-SHARE: COLLABORATE FOR UNDERSTANDING   105

VOCAB-O-GRAM   109

WORD SORT   115

WORD WALLS   119

Appendix   *123*

INSTRUCTIONAL STRATEGIES AND THE TOOLS THAT SUPPORT THEM

Builds Background Knowledge

CONCEPT LADDER	19
CONCEPTS AND VOCABULARY: CATEGORIES AND LABELS	25
DICTOGLOS	35
FOCUSED CLOZE	39
FRAYER MODEL	43
LEAD	63
LIST-GROUP-LABEL	69
POSSIBLE QUESTIONS	75
POSSIBLE SENTENCES	81
VOCAB-O-GRAM	109
WORD SORT	115

Teaches Words That Are Critical to Comprehension

FRAYER MODEL   43

SEMANTIC FEATURE ANALYSIS   91

THINK-PAIR-SHARE: COLLABORATE FOR UNDERSTANDING   105

Provides Support During Reading and Writing

CONCEPT CIRCLES   13

CONCEPT LADDER   19

CONCEPTS AND VOCABULARY: CATEGORIES AND LABELS   25

FREQUENT CONTACT   49

LEAD   63

POSSIBLE QUESTIONS   75

POSSIBLE SENTENCES   81

SEMANTIC FEATURE ANALYSIS   91

SEMANTIC MAPPING   97

WORD WALLS   119

Develops Conceptual Framework for Themes, Topics, and Units of Study

CONCEPT CIRCLES   13

CONCEPTS AND VOCABULARY: CATEGORIES AND LABELS   25

CONTEXTUAL REDEFINITION   31

DICTOGLOS   35

FOCUSED CLOZE   39

LEAD   63

LIST-GROUP-LABEL   69

POSSIBLE QUESTIONS   75

POSSIBLE SENTENCES   81

PREVIEWING CONTENT VOCABULARY   87

SEMANTIC FEATURE ANALYSIS   91

SEMANTIC MAPPING   97

VOCAB-O-GRAM   109

WORD SORT   115

WORD WALLS   119

Assesses Students' Understanding of Words and Concepts

CONCEPT CIRCLES   13

CONCEPT LADDER   19

CONCEPTS AND VOCABULARY: CATEGORIES AND LABELS   25

CONTEXTUAL REDEFINITION   31

FOCUSED CLOZE   39

FREQUENT CONTACT   49

"I'M THINKING OF A WORD . . ."   55

I SPY: A WORD SCAVENGER HUNT   59

LEAD   63

LIST-GROUP-LABEL   69

POSSIBLE QUESTIONS   75

POSSIBLE SENTENCES   81

PREVIEWING CONTENT VOCABULARY   87

SEMANTIC FEATURE ANALYSIS   91

SEMANTIC MAPPING   97

SURVIVAL OF THE FITTEST   101

THINK-PAIR-SHARE: COLLABORATE FOR UNDERSTANDING   105

VOCAB-O-GRAM   109

WORD SORT   115

ACKNOWLEDGMENTS

I am grateful to the students and teachers who use the instructional strategies I highlight in my writing. Now that I am out of my own classroom, these teachers and students provide the reality check for the work I do. Their ideas for adaptations and creative applications always make my ideas more relevant for a wider range of classrooms.

As always, I am also grateful to have found a home in the Stenhouse family. Philippa Stratton continues to be the just-right editor for my writing. She is patient, thoughtful, and resourceful. She treats authors and their words with respect and always looks for the kernels of writing that are central to our ideas. From the time I have an idea until the book is in the hands of educators, each member of the Stenhouse team contributes in making my writing something I am proud to own. I am thankful to each of them.

INTRODUCTION

One must be drenched in words, literally soaked in them, to
have the right ones form themselves into the proper pattern at
the right moment.

—HART CRANE

Why another book on teaching vocabulary? I have pondered that question several times in the course of writing this book. When I wrote *Words, Words, Words: Teaching Vocabulary in Grades 4–12* in 1999, I began the first chapter with a quote from Baumann and Kame'enui: "We know too much to say we know too little, and we know too little to say that we know enough. Indeed language is difficult to put into words" (1991, 604). Since I wrote that book eight years ago, there have been many books and research studies highlighting the role of effective vocabulary instruction in reading, writing, and critical thinking. Yet, as I work in schools and classrooms across the country, I continue to see teachers and students struggling to find ways to make content vocabulary accessible and meaningful. The research is there but the classroom application for that research is still in its infancy.

In 2004, I wrote *Tools for Teaching Content Literacy* in order to help teachers implement effective literacy instruction in the schools where I was part of their professional development. It was designed so teachers could take research on effective strategies and see models for what that research might look like in their classrooms. I highlighted the original researchers and explained the strategies. I then showed examples of those strategies as they were used in a variety of content classrooms. I focused less on vocabulary than on other instructional strategies because *Words, Words, Words* was available and the vocabulary instruction I wrote about in that book was applicable to all content areas.

Since the publication of *Words, Words, Words*, I have become increasingly aware of how significant vocabulary instruction is in content classrooms. Students seldom bring background knowledge that will help them successfully negotiate their content reading. In *Building Background Knowledge for Academic Achievement: Research on What Works in Schools* (2004), Marzano makes a case for increasing building background knowledge by increasing the emphasis on vocabulary instruction: "the research and theory strongly suggest that teaching vocabulary is synonymous with teaching background knowledge. The packets of information that constitute our background knowledge all have labels associated with them" (35). As I studied this research, I was struck by the exponential impact of teaching students academic vocabulary as a way to increase word knowledge and background knowledge. Learners would not only know more about the content, but they would also know the language used inside the content.

Inside Words combines current research on effective vocabulary instruction similar to the research highlighted in *Words, Words, Words* with effective instructional strategies similar to those highlighted in *Tools for Teaching Content Literacy*. It also joins the two formats: I blended the quick overview format from *Tools* with several classrooms examples, as I did in *Words*. Baumann and Kame'enui's words are indeed true: "We know too much to say we know too little." Although we still may not know *all* we need to know about vocabulary instruction, we do know a great deal about what effective vocabulary instruction could look like in content classrooms. It is my hope that this book will help support your effective classroom instruction with vocabulary research and instructional strategies.

Why Teach Vocabulary?

Most educators believe that vocabulary instruction is critical in any classroom. The issue is not whether we should have vocabulary instruction, but how to make that vocabulary instruction have meaning beyond assigned word lists. Most of us have struggled and continue to puzzle over how to teach vocabulary in meaningful and memorable ways so our students have access to the words in their reading, writing, and thinking. In *Building Academic Vocabulary Teacher's Manual*, Marzano and Pickering highlight the connection between vocabulary knowledge and comprehension of content:

> *People's knowledge of any topic is encapsulated in the terms they know that are relevant to the topic. The more students understand these terms, the easier it is for them to understand information they may read or hear about the topic. The more terms a person knows about a given subject, the easier it is to understand—and learn—new information related to that subject. (2005, 2–3)*

The why of vocabulary instruction is easily answered: in the absence of a repertoire of effective instructional strategies for teaching those words that are critical to students' understanding of a variety of texts, they will continue to struggle in their content classes. It is a cycle all too familiar to most of us.

At one time or another, we have all complained that our students can't or won't read their text assignments. Regardless of how aesthetically appealing publishers make content textbooks, the fact remains that most students bring little background knowledge of or interest in the concepts and related vocabulary they will encounter in their assigned reading. Relevant research findings are listed in the chart that follows. One important finding is research that understanding some content vocabulary is critical to comprehending a text. Moore, Readence, and Rickelman build on Readence, Bean, and Baldwin's (1985) position that students need to become *insiders* in their interaction with content reading:

> *Outsiders are restricted in their communication with a group because they cannot use the group's special vocabulary and the concepts inherent in that terminology. Insiders use special vocabulary freely to communicate with the collective members of a group. (Moore, Readance, and Rickelman 1989, 36)*

In an effort to help students gain this *insider* position in relation to content reading and writing, teachers often choose the most challenging words for preteaching. In spite of that practice, many students are still unable (or unwilling) to read their texts and do not use the content terminology in their writing and speaking.

Students agree with teachers that content vocabulary is a roadblock to learning content. When questioned about reading their textbook assignments, students reported that one of the greatest challenges in reading these texts or completing writing assignments in content classes is that they don't know the vocabulary words. In research studies I've conducted, students always report that the difficulty of the vocabulary makes reading their textbooks impossible. On a recent survey, I asked students how these challenging words were taught in their classes; the most frequent response was that they were given a list of words when they started a new chapter in the textbook. They were asked to copy

WHAT DO WE KNOW FROM RESEARCH?

Knowledge of word meaning is critical to success in reading.	Johnson, Toms-Bronowski, and Pittelman 1983; Barrett and Graves 1981; Becker 1977; Davis 1972; Hunt 1957
A rich conceptual base matters.	Johnson and Pearson 1984
Children learn language through ordinary exposure and instruction.	Beck, McKeown, and Kucan 2002
Students learn words in a variety of ways.	Blachowicz and Fisher 2004; Beck and McKeown 1991; Cunningham and Stanovich 1991; Nagy 1988
Students learn words through wide reading.	Nagy and Herman 1987; Fielding, Wilson, and Anderson 1986
Students learn new words by learning strategies for understanding unfamiliar words.	Blachowicz and Fisher 2004; Nagy 1988; Dale and O'Rourke 1986
Language/word awareness is critical to learning new words.	Cooper 2006; Anderson and Nagy 1992; Beck and McKeown 1983
Prior knowledge/experience supports increased vocabulary knowledge.	Marzano 2004; Mezynski 1983; Anderson and Freebody 1981
There is a relationship between difficulty of words in text and comprehension.	Graves 1986; Anderson and Freebody 1981
Direct vocabulary instruction improves comprehension.	Baumann, Kame'enui, and Ash 2003; Beck and McKeown 1991; Stahl and Fairbanks 1986
ESL students rely more heavily on direct instruction than native speakers.	Goulden, Nation, and Read 1990
Context clues vary in degree of "helpfulness" to readers.	Beck, McKeown, and McCaslin 1983
Knowing a word means more than knowing a definition for the word.	Scott and Nagy 1997; Dale and O'Rourke 1986
Repeated exposure to words in meaningful contexts improves comprehension.	Nagy 1990; Eller, Pappas, and Brown 1988; McKeown et al. 1985; Beck, Perfetti, and McKeown 1982
Discussion leads to vocabulary learning.	Stahl and Clark 1987; Stahl and Vancil 1986
Semantic mapping improves recall and understanding.	Pittelman, Levin, and Johnson 1985; Johnson, Toms-Bronowski, and Pittelman 1982
Teaching word parts improves recall and understanding.	White, Sowell, and Yanagihara 1989; Dale and O'Rourke 1986; Fry, Fountoukidis, and Polk 1985
Instruction toward Tier 2 words can be most productive.	Beck and McKeown 1985

the words and find a definition for each word from the dictionary or textbook glossary and then use the target words in a sentence. Not surprisingly, students reported remembering or really knowing few of these words. So, how can we overcome this ongoing dilemma?

How Do We Describe Effective Vocabulary Instruction?

When I was in my own classroom, I used to say that I wasn't sure how to define effective vocabulary instruction but I sure knew what it looked like when it was happening. On those days when effective vocabulary instruction was occurring, the joy students experienced in seeing a word they knew in a new context, or being able to use interesting and specialized vocabulary in their writing, was palpable in our classroom. On other days, every aspect of vocabulary instruction was a challenge.

In Beck, McKeown and Kucan's book, *Bringing Words to Life: Robust Vocabulary Instruction*, the authors highlight characteristics of robust vocabulary instruction. Instruction that meets their definition of robust provides the following:

- Rich information about words and their uses;
- Frequent and varied opportunities for students to think about and use words; and,
- Enhanced student language comprehension and production. (2002, 2)

After reading the authors' definition of robust instruction, I began gathering tools for content teachers to use with their students in order to make the concepts and vocabulary meaningful, memorable, and useful. When these tools are used appropriately by matching the instructional strategy with the goal, teachers discover that not only does comprehension increase, but also academic writing is more precise, logical, and interesting.

How *Inside Words* Is Organized

After describing and illustrating the strategies in this book, I was left with the decision of how to organize them to be helpful and easily accessible to educators. My first thought was to use traditional categories of pre-, during, and post-reading; however, as I tried to categorize, I kept encountering the same dilemma: instructional strategies such as LEAD are effective pre-reading strategies, but they also support comprehension and provide a structure for students to demonstrate understanding post-reading.

I then decided to organize the strategies based on components of a comprehensive vocabulary program as described in *Vocabulary Instruction: Research to Practice* (Baumann and Kame'enui 2004). In this research-based approach to effective classroom practices, the authors cite four components of comprehensive vocabulary instruction:

- fostering word consciousness;
- teaching individual words;
- teaching strategies for learning words independently; and,
- presenting frequent/extensive/varied opportunities for independent reading.

Once again, I was faced with a dilemma: the strategies all foster word consciousness and highlight individual words or concepts, and all employ diverse texts as a way to demonstrate words used in a meaningful context. I didn't want the organizational categories to limit the ways teachers might apply these tools, yet using either of these two systems could lead educators to see the strategies as single-purpose instructional tools.

I finally chose to organize them alphabetically so they could be easily found for teaching as well as for discussion in study groups or professional development. These are tools for teachers, and the purpose of a tool is to help get a job finished. So the strategies are in alphabetical order, and following the Table of Contents, there is a list that categorizes them into instructional strategies based on the ways I think they help students learn and use academic and specialized vocabulary. These instructional strategies are the following:

Builds background knowledge

Teaches words that are critical to comprehension

Provides support during reading and writing

Develops conceptual framework for themes, topics, and units of study

Assesses students' understanding of words and concepts

As you examine and use these teaching and learning tools in your classroom with your students, I hope you find that your robust instruction leads students to *insider* terminology—terminology that will help them think, talk, and write about their content knowledge so they can live and learn inside words.

References

Anderson, R. C., and P. Freebody. 1981. "Vocabulary Knowledge." In *Comprehension and Teaching: Research Reviews*, ed. J. Guthrie, 77–117. Newark, DE: International Reading Association.

Anderson, R. C., and W. E. Nagy. 1992. "The Vocabulary Conundrum." *American Educator* (Winter): 14–18, 44–47.

Barrett, M. T., and M. F. Graves. 1981. "A Vocabulary Program for Junior High School Remedial Readers." *Journal of Reading* 25 (November): 146–50.

Baumann, J. F., and E. J. Kame'enui. 1991. "Research on Vocabulary Instruction: Ode to Voltaire." In *Handbook on Teaching the English Language Arts*, eds. J. Flood, J. M. Jensen, D. Lapp, and J. R. Squire, 604–32. New York: Macmillan.

———, eds. 2004. *Vocabulary Instruction: Research to Practice*. New York: Guilford Press.

Baumann, J. F., E. J. Kame'enui, and G. E. Ash. 2003. "Research on Vocabulary Instruction: Voltaire Redux." In *Handbook of*

Research on Teaching the English Language Arts, eds. J. Flood, J. Jensen, D. Lapp, and J. R. Squire, 752–85. New York: Macmillan.

Beck, I., and M. McKeown. 1983. "Learning Words Well: A Program to Enhance Vocabulary and Comprehension." *The Reading Teacher* 36 (March): 622–25.

———. 1985. "Teaching Vocabulary: Making the Instruction Fit the Goal." *Educational Perspectives* 23 (1): 11–15.

———. 1991. "Conditions of Vocabulary Acquisition." In *Handbook of Reading Research*, Vol. 2, eds. R. Barr, M. Kamill, P. Mosentahl, and P. D. Pearson, 789–814. New York: Longman.

Beck, I. L., M. G. McKeown, and L. Kucan. 2002. *Bringing Words to Life: Robust Vocabulary Instruction*. New York: Guilford Press.

Beck, I., M. McKeown, and E. McCaslin. 1983. "All Contexts Are Not Created Equal." *Elementary School Journal* 83: 177–81.

Beck, I. L., C. A. Perfetti, and M. G. McKeown. 1982. "Effects of Long-Term Vocabulary Instruction on Lexical Access and Reading Comprehension." *Journal of Educational Psychology* 74: 506–21.

Becker, W. C. 1977. "Teaching Reading and Language to the Disadvantaged: What We Have Learned from Field Research." *Harvard Edcuational Review* 47: 518–43.

Blachowicz, C. L. Z., and P. Fisher. 2004. "Keep the 'Fun' in Fundamental: Encouraging Word Awareness and Incidental Word Learning in the Classroom Through Word Play." In *Vocabulary Instruction: Research to Practice*, eds. J. F. Baumann and E. J. Kame'enui, 218–37. New York: Guilford Press.

Cooper, J. D. 2006. *Literacy: Helping Children Construct Meaning*. 6th ed. Boston: Houghton Mifflin.

Cunningham, A. E., and K. E. Stanovich. 1991. "Tracking the Unique Effects of Print Exposure in Children: Associations with Vocabulary, General Knowledge, and Spelling." *Journal of Educational Psychology* 83: 264–74.

Dale, E., and J. O'Rourke. 1986. *Vocabulary Building: A Process Approach*. Columbus, OH: Zaner-Bloser.

Davis, F. B. 1972. "Psychometric Research on Comprehension in Reading." *Reading Research Quarterly* 7 (4): 628–78.

Eller, R. G., C. C. Pappas, and E. Brown. 1988. "The Lexical Development of Kindergarteners: Learning from Written Context." *Journal of Reading Behavior* 20 (1): 5–24.

Fielding, L. G., P. T. Wilson, and R. C. Anderson. 1986. "A New Focus on Free Reading: The Role of Tradebooks in Reading Instruction." In *Contexts of School-Based Literacy*, ed. T. E. Raphael, 149–60. New York: Random House.

Fry, E. B., D. L. Fountoukidis, and J. K. Polk. 1985. *The New Reading Teacher's Book of Lists*. Englewood Cliffs, NJ: Prentice-Hall.

Goulden, R., P. Nation, and J. Read. 1990. "How Large Can a Receptive Vocabulary Be?" *Applied Linguistics* 11: 341–63.

Graves, M. F. 1986. "Vocabulary Learning and Instruction." In *Review of Research in Education*, Vol. 13, eds. E. Z. Rothkopf and L. C. Ehri, 49–89. Washington, DC: American Educational Research Association.

Hunt, C. L., Jr. 1957. "Can We Measure Specific Factors Associated with Reading Comprehension?" *Journal of Educational Research* 51: 161–71.

Johnson, D. D., and P. D. Pearson. 1984. *Teaching Reading Vocabulary*. 2nd ed. New York: Holt, Rinehart and Winston.

Johnson, D. D., S. Toms-Bronowski, and S. D. Pittelman. 1982. *An Investigation of the Effectiveness of Semantic Mapping and Semantic Feature Analysis with Intermediate Grade Children*. Program Report 8303. Madison: Wisconsin Center for Educational Research, University of Wisconsin.

———. 1983. "Fundamental Factors in Reading Comprehension Revisited." In *Reading Research Revisited*, eds. L. Gentile and M. Kamil. Columbus, OH: Charles Merrill.

Marzano, R. J. 2004. *Building Background Knowledge for Academic Achievement: Research on What Works in Schools*. Alexandria, VA: Association for Supervision and Curriculum Development.

Marzano, R. J., and D. J. Pickering. 2005. *Building Academic Vocabulary Teacher's Manual*. Alexandria, VA: Association for Supervision and Curriculum Development.

McKeown, M. G., I. L. Beck, R. C. Omanson, and M. T. Pople. 1985. "Some Effects of the Nature and Frequency of Vocabulary Instruction on the Knowledge and Use of Words." *Reading Research Quarterly* 20: 522–35.

Mezynski, K. 1983. "Issues Concerning the Acquisition of Knowledge: Effects of Vocabulary Training on Reading Comprehension." *Review of Educational Research* 53: 253–79.

Moore, D. W., J. E. Readence, and R. J. Rickelman. 1989. *Prereading Activities for Content Area Reading and Learning.* 2nd ed. Newark, DE: International Reading Association.

Nagy, W. 1988. *Teaching Vocabulary to Improve Reading Comprehension.* Newark, DE: International Reading Association.

Nagy, W. E., and P. A. Herman. 1987. "Breadth and Depth of Vocabulary Knowledge: Implications for Acquisition and Instruction." In *The Nature of Vocabulary Acquisition*, eds. M. G. McKeown and M. E. Curtis, 19–35. Hillsdale, NJ: Erlbaum.

Pittelman, S. D., K. M. Levin, and D. D. Johnson. 1985. *An Investigation of Two Instructional Settings in the Use of Semantic Mapping with Poor Readers.* Program Report No. 85-4. Madison: Wisconsin Center for Educational Research, University of Wisconsin.

Readence, J. E., T. W. Bean, and R. S. Baldwin. 1985. *Content Area Reading: An Integrated Approach.* 2nd ed. Dubuque, IA: Kendall/Hunt.

Scott, J. A., and W. Nagy. 1997. "Understanding the Definitions of Unfamiliar Verbs." *Reading Research Quarterly* 32 (2): 184–200.

Stahl, S. A. 1987. "Three Principles of Effective Vocabulary Instruction." *Journal of Reading* 29: 662–68.

Stahl, S. A., and C. H. Clark. 1987. "The Effects of Participatory Expectations in Classroom Discussion on the Learning of Science Vocabulary." *American Educational Research Journal* 24 (4): 541–55.

Stahl, S. A., and M. M. Fairbanks. 1986. "The Effects of Vocabulary Instruction: A Model-Based Meta-analysis." *Review of Educational Research* 56 (1): 72–110.

Stahl, S. A., and S. J. Vancil. 1986. "Discussion Is What Makes Semantic Maps Work." *The Reading Teacher* 40: 62–67.

White, T. G., J. Sowell, and A. Yanagihara. 1989. "Teaching Elementary Students to Use Word-Part Clues." *The Reading Teacher* 42: 302–08.

CONCEPT CIRCLES

What Are Concept Circles?

Concept Circles (Vacca, Vacca, and Gove 1987) are circles with words placed in sections of the circle. While many variations occur during the use of Concept Circles, the basic structure is usually the same: a circle with four sections; each section contains a word or phrase. The basic structure works for a variety of instructional and assessment purposes.

How Do They Work?

Concept Circles can work in a variety of ways and can be used for many purposes. At its most basic level, a Concept Circle gives students an opportunity to categorize words and justify the connections between and among the words. A circle is divided into four equal sections. Each section of the circle contains a word or phrase that you would like your students to think, talk, and/or write about. Several possible scenarios are listed here highlighting how Concept Circles could work.

1. Put words or phrases in each section of the circle and ask students to write about the connections they see between the words and phrases. Why are these words in a Concept Circle together?
2. Put vocabulary words in three of the sections of the circle. Students add a word in the fourth section and then write about why they chose that word to add and how the words in the circle form a concept.
3. Ask students to choose four vocabulary words from their study of a topic or a text and use those four words to write about what they have learned about the topic. These can be teacher- or student-generated lists of words.
4. Ask students to shade either the words that go together or the word that doesn't fit with the others. Students can then talk or write about what attributes caused a word to be included or excluded.

When and Why Would I Use This Strategy?

You would use this instructional tool when you would like students to participate in conceptual thinking about content vocabulary. Concept Circles can be used to help focus students' discussions, to review word meanings and word families, and to provide support for students' writing.

I most often use Concept Circles as an assessment tool. In the first example from a sixth-grade classroom, the teacher has chosen words students have encountered in their reading about the Westward movement. The students are then using the words to help them write a focused summary of what they have learned so far in the unit. The additional Concept Circle examples have been used as a post-reading

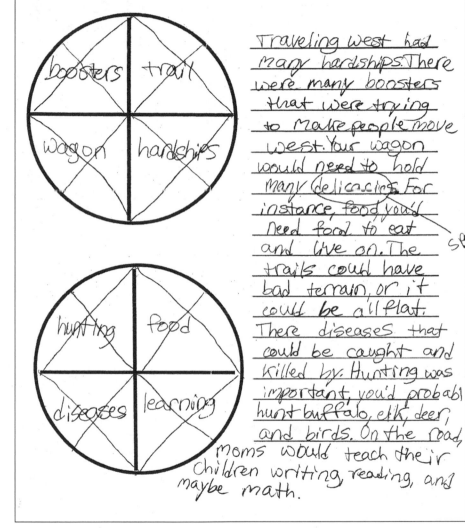

CONCEPT CIRCLES ASSESSMENT

Explain the concepts and connections.

Concept circle 1 (top): boosters, trail, wagon, hardships

Concept circle 2 (bottom): hunting, food, diseases, learning

Traveling west had many hardships. There were many boosters that were trying to make people move west. Your wagon would need to hold many delicacies. For instance, food you'd need food to eat and live on. The trails could have bad terrain, or it could be all flat. There diseases that could be caught and killed by. Hunting was important, you'd probabl hunt buffalo, elk, deer, and birds. On the road, moms would teach their children writing, reading, and maybe math.

Example 1

assessment. The second example has been given to students after they completed reading Act I of *Romeo and Juliet*. Example three is a post-reading assessment of students' comprehension after reading a book in the History of US series (Hakim 1999). In all cases, the teacher is using Concept Circles to assess content knowledge.

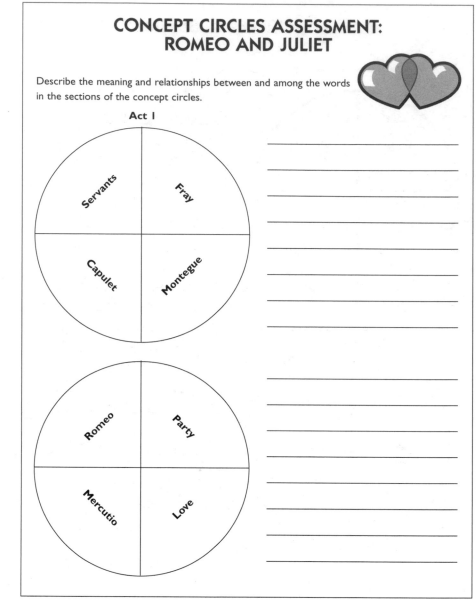

CONCEPT CIRCLES ASSESSMENT: ROMEO AND JULIET

Describe the meaning and relationships between and among the words in the sections of the concept circles.

Act I

Servants | Fray

Capulet | Montegue

Romeo | Party

Mercutio | Love

Example 2

Research/Origins/Further Reading

Allen, J. (1999). *Words, Words, Words: Teaching Vocabulary in Grades 4–12.* Portland, ME: Stenhouse.

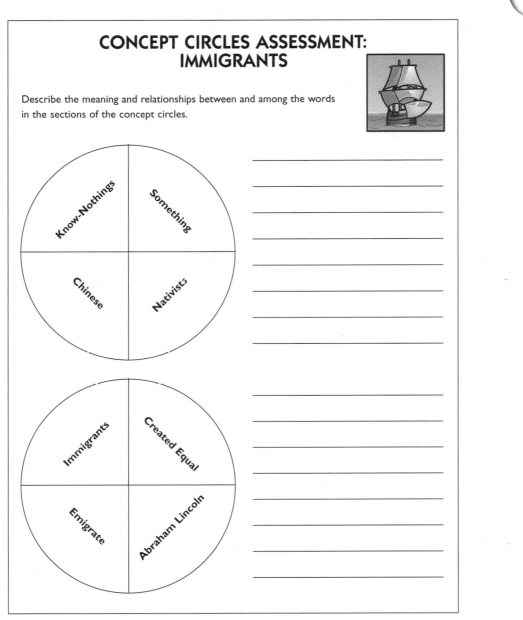

CONCEPT CIRCLES ASSESSMENT: IMMIGRANTS

Describe the meaning and relationships between and among the words in the sections of the concept circles.

Know-Nothings · Something · Chinese · Nativists

Immigrants · Created Equal · Emigrate · Abraham Lincoln

Example 3

Hakim, J. 1999. *Liberty for All? 1800–1860*. 2nd ed. A History of US series, Book 5. New York: Oxford University Press.

Vacca, J. L., R. T. Vacca, and M. K. Gove. 1987. *Reading and Learning to Read*. Boston: Little, Brown.

CONCEPT
LADDER

What Is a Concept Ladder?

Concept Ladders (Gillet and Temple 1986/1982) are a teaching tool that can help students explain and describe their understandings of a complex word or concept. Concept Ladders are based on students' responses to teacher or student-generated questions about the word or concept. The first three categories of questions (kind, part, stage) that teachers or students might generate are based on Upton's (1973) work with semantics. The fourth category of questions, product, is Gillet and Temple's (1986) extension of Upton's work. These questions center on four areas of knowing a word:

1. Kind: What is it a kind of or what are kinds of it?
2. Part: What is it part of or what are its parts?
3. Stage: What is it a stage of or what are its stages?
4. Product: What is it a product of or what are products of it?

How Do Concept Ladders Work?

Unlike a word of the day, which may be connected to a single experience with the word and its definition, a Concept Ladder focuses on a big idea. Therefore, a Concept Ladder is best used for longer periods of time as part of a thematic or topical unit of study. The graphic organizer shown in Example 1 is being used over the course of reading several works related to intolerance.

1. In anticipation of the unit of study, students respond to the questions with their initial understandings of the theme or topic. As students think about and discuss causes and effects of intolerance, they are focused on knowing the concept at the *product/stage* levels. When discussing language and words associated with intolerance, they are focused on knowing the concept at the *part* level. As they brainstorm historical and contemporary examples of intolerance, they are focused on the *kind* level of knowing the word. The final questions related to evidence of and connections made to the concept require students to synthesize their understandings of the concept using all four levels of knowing a word.

2. After reading, discussion, and viewing, students revisit the concept ladder and add subquestions in each of the categories. For example, under the category Causes of, students added: What caused the Rock Springs Massacre? How does the cause of the Internment Camps fit the word *intolerance*?

3. Throughout and at the end of the unit of study, students use the Concept Ladder and their questions/responses for academic writing related to the theme/topic.

CONCEPT LADDER

Concept:	**Intolerance**

Causes of?

Effects of?

Language associated with?

Words that mean the same as?

Historical examples of?

Contemporary examples of?

Evidence of?

Literature/reading connections made?

Adapted from J. W. Gillet and C. Temple (1986)

Example 1

When and Why Would I Use a Concept Ladder?

A Concept Ladder is an effective way for you and your students to assess and extend their understanding of a concept. Through guided discussion connecting the Concept Ladder questions to your study of the concept and students' understanding of the concept and its meaning, students come to know the concept at a level deeper than a definitional level. A Concept Ladder is best used with a big idea: themes, such as intolerance or justice; movements or time periods, such as the Renaissance or the sixties; political forces or structures, such as communism or the Common Market; or phenomena, such as metamorphosis or gravitational pull. Concept Ladders as constructed by Gillet and Temple typically provide the categories with spaces for students to write responses, as shown here:

Kind of: Part of: Stage of: Product of:

_____   _____   _____   _____

I have found it easier to create a visual ladder with students. In the Concept Ladder shown in Example 2, Danielle, a fourth grader, has started her own concept ladder prior to reading her science book. She has created categories of words related to body systems: cells, tissue, organs. From this initial word list, Danielle will then generate the questions she has about each in relation to body systems as she thinks about kinds, parts, stages, and products of body systems. All categories won't work with all concepts, so teaching students to explore the categories that are relevant is critical.

In the Concept Ladder on intolerance in Example 1, students have taken the four types of questions and created their own questions from those. These ninth-grade students are exploring the same generic categories of questions that Danielle will explore but have generated their questions related to intolerance.

As with any graphic organizer, the key is to adapt it to meet your instructional goals and the needs of your students. Using a Concept Ladder should support your students in considering the attributes of concepts in order to develop a deeper understanding of the concept's meaning.

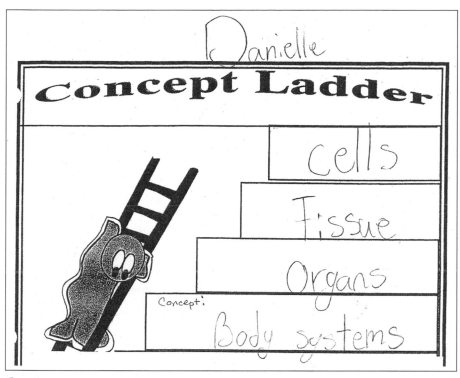

Example 2

Research/Origins/Further Reading

Allen, J. 1999. *Words, Words, Words: Teaching Vocabulary in Grades 4–12*. Portland, ME: Stenhouse.

Allen, J., and C. Landaker. 2004. *Reading History: A Practical Guide to Improving Literacy*. New York: Oxford University Press.

Gillet, J. W., and C. Temple. 1986. *Understanding Reading Problems: Assessment and Instruction*. 2nd ed. Boston: Little, Brown.

Upton, A. 1973. *Design for Thinking: A First Book on Semantics*. Palo Alto, CA: Pacific Press.

CONCEPTS AND VOCABULARY: CATEGORIES AND LABELS

What Is Concepts and Vocabulary: Categories and Labels?

Concepts and Vocabulary: Categories and Labels is based on findings showing that the most researched and validated studies are those focused on students' organizing information (Nist and Simpson 2000). This activity gives students the opportunity to think about a cluster of technical vocabulary words that will be used in upcoming reading. Given a list of words (concepts and vocabulary), students categorize and label the words based on common attributes.

How Does It Work?

In this activity, teachers choose important technical vocabulary that would be critical to students' comprehension of content or a text. These words are placed in a word bank for students. Once the key concepts and critical vocabulary have been chosen, the format for the activity is as follows:

1. Provide each student with a copy of the key concepts and critical vocabulary.
2. Read each of the terms aloud as students follow to match pronunciation to print.
3. Allow students to ask questions and remind them of places where they can find additional information about the words (texts, websites, resources, etc.).
4. Assign student groups.
5. Ask groups to discuss the words and decide on how to categorize the word into logical groups.
6. Give each category a label.
7. Ask students to justify their word groups and labels.

When and Why Would I Use This Strategy?

Concepts and Vocabulary: Categories and Labels supports several significant literacy goals. Students are accessing and gaining background knowledge related to the topic based on encountering the technical vocabulary related to the topic. In addition, by discussing and grouping the words into categories, students are creating attributes of the words in relation to each other and the topic being studied. In labeling the words, students create a structure for remembering the words and the information they have gathered related to the words.

In Example 1, the science teacher is using the word bank (see the Possible Questions tool for an alternative activity) related to an upcoming study of viruses and bacteria. Students will discuss these technical

---

CONCEPTS AND VOCABULARY: CATEGORIES AND LABELS

Read and think about each of the words you have been given. Now, group the words into categories that make logical sense to you. Ask yourself which words would logically go together. After you group the words, give each group a label. Be ready to explain or justify the rationale behind your groups and labels.

Words:

medicine	Legionella	microorganisms	walls
spiral	strep throat	microbes	salmonella
cytoplasm	E. coli	rodlike	decomposers
genetic	bacteria	food poisoning	ribosomes
antibiotics	invade	spherical	healthy

Example 1

words related to the topic and then group words into categories. Students can perform this activity using a graphic format as seen here or the teacher can provide groups of students with cards so students can physically move the cards into groups. Some categories typically generated by students include parts of cells, shapes of viruses/bacteria, things

CONCEPTS AND VOCABULARY: CATEGORIES AND LABELS
Firebug

Read and think about each of the words you have been given. Now, group the words into categories that make logical sense to you. Ask yourself which words would logically go together. After you group the words, give each group a label. Be ready to explain or justify the rationale behind your groups and labels.

Words:

blaze	smoldering	Tucson
Sedona	suspicious	embers
dude	vortex	fire extinguisher
crystals	radio	guest ranch
Red Rock Mountains	reporter	housekeeping
hidden treasures	cache	hermit
news anchor		

Example 2

that make you sick, things that help cure the symptoms, and words that describe viruses and bacteria.

These words came from a science lesson, but the instructional strategy is appropriate for any content area. In a reading class, a middle school teacher who is about to read *Firebug* (Mitchell 2004) might use the words listed in Example 2 for the Concepts and Vocabulary activity. Students would categorize these words with labels such as the following: words related to fire, places people live in the book, words related to treasures, jobs people had in the book. The graphic organizer shown in Example 1 can be used for students to develop their categories and create their labels. It is important to note with students that there are no set numbers of categories nor are there set numbers of words that go in each category.

Following this activity, the teacher can ask students to use their labels to create questions they believe will be answered in the text or create an outline with headings and subheadings. Either activity extends the initial vocabulary activity into support for comprehension.

Research/Origins/Further Reading

McCagg, E. C., and D. F. Dansereau. 1991. "A Convergent Paradigm for Examining Knowledge Mapping as a Learning Strategy." *Journal of Educational Research* 84: 317–24.

Mitchell, M. 2004. *Firebug*. Honesdale, PA: Boyds Mills Press.

Nist, S. L., and M. L. Simpson. 2000. "College Studying." In Vol. 3, *Handbook of Reading Research*, eds. M. L. Kamil, P. B. Mosenthal, P. D. Pearson, and R. Barr, 645–66. Mahwah, NJ: Lawrence Erlbaum.

CONTEXTUAL REDEFINITION

What Is Contextual Redefinition?

Contextual Redefinition (Cunningham, Cunningham, and Arthur 1981) is a teaching strategy that helps students learn the importance of context clues in understanding the meaning of a word or concept. Contextual Redefinition provides a way to introduce new vocabulary words to your students and gives students the opportunity to use a variety of context clues to predict and verify meanings. While context clues, when used alone, are not often a reliable source of word meaning (Shatz and Baldwin 1986; Nagy, Herman, and Anderson 1985; Deighton 1959), knowing how and when to use the clues that are in the text is a critical step toward students independently increasing their vocabulary.

How Does It Work?

Context clues, when used alone, are an unreliable source of word meaning; however, when combined with definitions, the combination is more significant than either used alone. Contextual Redefinition has the following instructional steps:

1. The teacher selects words that will occur in upcoming reading but are unfamiliar to students. In the example I'm using here (*The Last Book in the Universe*, [Philbrick 2000]), many of the words are unfamiliar or familiar but have new/unusual meanings because it is science fiction.

2. Each of the words is presented to students in isolation with local context (rest of the sentence in which the word appears) missing. I usually provide students with a list of about ten words. For example, unfamiliar or multiple meaning words from the first chapter of this novel include sexbos, trendies, wheel, urb, gummy, mope, bust him down, proov, mindprobes, and latch.

3. Students make predictions about possible meanings for the words based on their background knowledge and knowledge of word parts.

4. Students are then provided with the context for each of the words to determine context clues that are helpful for confirming or determining word meanings for the target words. As they use context for word meaning, students should cite which context clues (antonyms/synonyms; local context; structural analysis—word parts, background knowledge; or global context—beyond sentence-level) helped them determine word meaning. For example, this is the beginning text that includes some of the words in the target word list:

If you're reading this, it must be a thousand years from now. Because nobody around here reads anymore. Why bother, when you can just probe it? Put all the images and excitement right inside your brain and let it rip. There are all kinds of mindprobes—trendies, shooters, sexbos, whatever you want to

CONTEXTUAL REDEFINITION

Work with a group to make predictions for definitions of each of the following words. The words included here are found in _____. Remember that some words which look familiar will probably have new meanings in this context.

Word	Predicted Definition	Definition Based on Context	Context Clues Used
sexbos			
trendies			
wheel			
urb			
gummy			
mope			
bust him down			
proov			
mindprobes			
latch			

Based on this activity, I've learned the following strategies for determining word meaning through context clues:

experience. Shooters are violent, and trendies are about living in Eden, and sexbos, well you can guess what sexbos are about. They say probing is better than anything. I wouldn't know because I've got this serious medical condition that means I'm allergic to electrode needles. Stick one of those in my brain and it'll kick off a really bad seizure and then total mind melt, lights out, that's all, folks. (Philbrick 2000, 7–9)

When and Why Would I Use This Instructional Strategy?

This instructional strategy is appropriate for teaching students how to use context clues and definitions to solidify knowledge of word meanings. It would be appropriate to use this type of strategy every few weeks with a new novel or unit of study. This activity provides opportunities for students to predict word meanings and practice using each of the types of context clues to determine word meaning.

Research/Origins/Further Reading:

Cunningham, J. W., P. M. Cunningham, and S. V. Arthur. 1981. *Middle and Secondary School Reading.* New York: Longman.

Deighton, D. 1959. *Vocabulary Development in the Classroom.* New York: Bureau of Publications, Teachers College, Columbia University.

Irvin, J. L. 1990. *Reading and the Middle School Student: Strategies to Enhance Literacy.* Boston: Allyn and Bacon.

Nagy, W., P. Herman, and R. C. Anderson. 1985. "Learning Words from Context." *Reading Research Quarterly* 20: 233–53.

Philbrick, R. 2000. *The Last Book in the Universe.* New York: Blue Sky Press/Scholastic.

Shatz, E. K., and R. S. Baldwin. 1986. "Context Clues Are Unreliable Predictors of Word Meanings." *Reading Research Quarterly* 21: 429–53.

DICTOGLOS

What Is the Dictoglos Strategy?

Dictoglos is another term for grammar dictation (Wajnryb 1990). It is an instructional tool designed to support language learners in order to help them refine their understanding of language used in a text passage. The instructional strategy involves repeated dictations of short, dense text so students can recognize and record familiar words. Each student then pools his or her words with those of other learners in order to reconstruct the text. Dictoglos serves as a vehicle for students and teachers to assess how grammar works in a text.

How Does It Work?

At first glance, Dictoglos could be seen as a simple dictation where students listen and re-create what they hear. However, there are two purposes for Dictoglos: student recognition of familiar language and refinement of students' ability to work with others to reconstruct a version of the text from their shared lists of words. This occurs in a consistent series of instructional steps:

1. The teacher chooses a short text to read to students.
2. The teacher reads the text twice at a normal speed and students note any words or phrases that are familiar to them.
3. Students work in pairs of small groups to share their lists of words and phrases.
4. Students then use words and phrases noted by group members in order to reconstruct a version of the text they were read.
5. Students are then given a copy of the text and asked to compare their versions to the original.
6. The teacher can then use students' versions of the text to discuss grammar and context of words in a passage.
7. The teacher can use Dictoglos to determine students' understandings and misunderstandings of the way language works. This will enable teachers to make thoughtful decisions about next steps for students.

When and Why Would I Use This Strategy?

This instructional strategy is particularly useful in providing English language learners with background for content reading. Students are exposed to content or text-specific vocabulary words and given an opportunity to explore their meaning and use with their peers. The teacher then has the opportunity to assess where students might need more support.

In the example, "Do We Still Have Dragons?" the teacher is using a text she has written to use as part of Dictoglos. Students will be reading

DICTOGLOS
Do We Still Have Dragons?

Words/Phrases	Group Words/Phrases
Group Version of Text	**Compare to Original Text**

Do We Still Have Dragons?

We do have dragons but you will have to take a long trip to see them as they usually live on the Indonesian Islands. When you get there, you might discover that these dragons aren't quite like the dragons you have read about or seen in movies. These dragons are called Komodo dragons and they are actually the world's largest lizard. They can be over 10 feet long and weigh nearly 200 pounds. That's a big lizard!

I would want answers to lots of questions before visiting their home or natual habitat. I would want to know what Komodo dragons eat and whether they eat people or not. Are these dragons rare or are they common? If they are rare, are they on the endangered species list? Could I see one in a zoo or would I have to go to Indonesia? What questions would you have before searching for a Komodo dragon?

a longer text from *On the Trail of the Komodo Dragon* (Myers 1999). The teacher has rewritten a short portion of the text as a way to introduce students to content they will encounter in a future reading of the complete text. The text is read at a normal speed and then reread so students have two opportunities to write down words or phrases that are familiar to them. While individual words students note will vary, the words *dragon, lizards,* and *largest* almost always appear.

After each student creates an initial word bank from the oral reading of the text, they work in pairs or small groups to discuss and combine the words and phrases they have noted. After discussing the words and their understanding of the words, each group writes a group version of the text. In this way, students apply their knowledge of the words as well as the grammatical structures in which these words would be used in writing.

Students present their versions, and each group's version is compared to the original text. At this time, the teacher can clarify meanings for students and use their words to anticipate the content of the longer text.

Research/Origins/Further Reading

Myers, J. 1999. *On the Trail of the Komodo Dragon.* Honesdale, PA: Boyds Mills Press.

Wajnryb, R. 1990. *Grammar Dictation.* New York: Oxford University Press.

FOCUSED CLOZE

What Is the Focused Cloze Instructional Strategy?

Focused Cloze is a modification of the cloze procedure (Taylor 1953). The original cloze was designed as an assessment of text-to-reader readability match. In the cloze procedure a portion of text (two-hundred-fifty-plus words) is chosen. The beginning and ending of the excerpt remain intact, and then every *nth* word (fifth, seventh, tenth, etc.) is omitted. Words are omitted in a consistent pattern. Students use only the context to predict the omitted word. Words are considered correct if the word replacing the omitted word is an exact match. Scores above 60 percent correct indicate the text is at a student's independent level; scores between 40 to 60 percent correct indicate text is at an instructional level; scores below 40 percent correct indicate reading is at a frustration level.

Focused Cloze is a modification of this instructional strategy in that omitted words are those significant content terms you want students to use. Words are not omitted in a regular pattern; rather, words are chosen for omission from the text passage so students will encounter and learn content information. In addition, a word bank is provided for students so they can choose from among the listed words to complete the passage.

How Does It Work?

Focused Cloze can provide students with an opportunity to encounter specialized content words in a rich context. From that context, students can find information about the words as well as infer the word's properties. Words are provided so students' choices for completing the passage are limited to those content words in the word bank. In the example shown here, the teacher has used *Oh, Yikes! History's Grossest, Wackiest Moments* (Masoff 2006) to give students an opportunity to encounter content words related to a unit on prisons and punishment. The beginning and ending of the passage have been left intact; students supply the missing words to complete the passage using the word bank provided. In this way, students encounter the academic vocabulary connected to their unit on prisons and punishment prior to reading their textbook and other related texts. From this activity, the teacher can then have students highlight words that are still confusing or see if students can apply the words using the Possible Sentences or Possible Questions strategy.

When and Why Would I Use This Strategy?

The original cloze (Taylor 1953) was used as an assessment tool; Focused Cloze is used as a way to assess and build background

PRISONS AND PUNISHMENT

Think being grounded is a bummer? Try being marched out to the middle of the _____, tied up, and then _____ with sheep guts as your friends and neighbors gather to watch. Very embarrassing, not to mention smelly! But it could be worse. You could be grounded for *life*— sent to "the big house" (also known as prison, the _____, the pen the cooler, the joint, the pokey, the _____, the _____, the jug, and the stir)—a place where the bathrooms have no doors!

A Tooth for a Tooth

Early man's response to crime was simple. Get even! _____ was the respnse to wrongdoing. But as towns grew into cities, things started to get out of hand. We needed some rules! The first person to write down an _____ set of _____, with punishments for breaking those laws, was a fellow named _____ (*Hahm-uh-ROB-EE*). Hammurabi was a Mesopotamian _____ back in 1750 B.C.E. and was one of the first to come up with the idea of "an eye for an eye, a tooth for a tooth."

Painful Punishments

The ancient _____ and _____ figured that an ounce of _____ was worth a bucket of cutoff hands or noses. They developed strong _____, wrote _____ to protect their citizens, and developed _____ for crime. Do something wrong in ancient Greece and you'd be rowing your little hands raw in a slave galley in the middle of nowhere faster then you can say "Row, row, row your boat." The Romans' _____ for folks who misbehaved was a hungry, angry wild beast. Many criminals found themselves face to face with a famished lion. (Read more about battling beasts in GLADIATORS on page 104.)

Lock 'Em Up and Throw Away the Key

The Romans were among the first to create _____—really crummy, nasty places with bars on the windows and doors, and no hope for escape! They were called carcers (that's where our word "_____" comes from), and had dungeon-like cages built twelve feet underground. Since people were _____ to death for the teeniest things back then, the _____ wasn't used as a long-term prison—just a final damp _____.

Pay Up!

Jails didn't become _____ until the twelfth century in England, where King Henry II ordered every county sheriff to build a jail (or _____, as the English liked to spell it). One of England's scariest "gaols" was called Newgate. Every Monday morning, some of its prisoners were dragged out to the front yard where they were _____, _____, or even _____. These public _____ were supposed to scare other people away from committing crimes. You can bet it'd make you think twice about stealing!

People sent to "gaol" had to apply to get out and while they were behind bars they had to pay for their food. Sheriffs figured they had a _____ audience, so they charged a lot for the crummy food they served. Visiting friends or family members brought _____ to pay. It was either that or _____ to death.

continued on next page

Which Is Which?

Bet you don't know the difference between a _____ and a _____. A jail holds people awaiting trial and sentencing. After a person has been found guilty, he or she gets sent off to prison.

starve	prisons	solution	official
punishments	carcer	captive	solution
condemned	Romans	whipped	Greeks
revenge	gaol	pressed to death	death row
town square	Hammurabi	pelted	slammer
hoosegow	clink	laws	official
common	king	executions	governments
jail	prison	incarcerated	prevention
punishments	laws	hanged	coins

Adapted from J. Masoff (2006), Oh, Yikes! History's Grossest, Wackiest Moments. *New York: Workman*

knowledge in anticipation of content to be studied. You could use the procedure with an excerpt from your textbook, or you could use a supplemental text as long as the text you choose gives students the opportunity to encounter the content vocabulary critical to understanding the concepts you are teaching. This activity is highly engaging, and students enjoy reading, discussing the words, debating accurate choices, inferring information about the words, and seeing immediate applications for the words.

Research/Origins/Further Reading

Jacobson, J. M. 1998. *Content Area Reading: Integration with the Language Arts.* Albany, NY: Delmar.

Masoff, J. 2006. *Oh, Yikes! History's Grossest, Wackiest Moments.* New York: Workman.

Taylor, W. 1953. "Cloze Procedure: A New Tool for Measuring Readability." *Journalism Quarterly* 30: 415–33.

FRAYER MODEL

What Is the Frayer Model?

The Frayer Model is an instructional strategy teachers would use for helping students learn new concepts through the use of attributes and nonattributes. The Frayer Model has several steps where the teacher is helping students learn a concept by giving examples and nonexamples of the concept. Steps (originally seven) include the following:

1. Define the concept giving attributes of the concept.
2. Show students how this concept differs from other similar concepts (by highlighting noncritical attributes).
3. Provide examples and explain what makes these examples.

4. Provide nonexamples and explain what makes these nonexamples.
5. Provide students with examples and nonexamples and ask them to determine whether they are examples or nonexamples.

How Does the Frayer Model Work?

The Frayer Model is usually done with a critical concept that is part of a unit or theme. It is time-consuming and so would usually be revisited over several days of study. When using the Frayer Model, the teacher is directly teaching students about the concept by providing specific attributes/nonattributes and examples/nonexamples to refine students' definitions of the concept. In the example here, the English teacher is using the Frayer Model to teach her students the critical attributes of the word *zealot* prior to reading *Armageddon Summer* (Yolen and Coville 1998).

1. A *zealot* is someone who is filled with zeal (intense devotion or enthusiasm) for something. This word is usually given to someone who is so devoted to the cause that they can seem fanatical about it. A zealot is someone whose devotion is so great that it can seem to be excessive or irrational. The cause to which a zealot is devoted takes precedence over almost everything else in the person's life.

2. If you looked up the word *zealot* in a thesaurus, you might find synonyms like *supporter* or *believer*, but a zealot is more than a supporter or believer. Zealots believe in what they are doing and they support a cause, but they do so to an excessive degree. If we were looking at degrees of intensity, *believer* would be at the bottom and *zealot* would be over the top!

3. We often think of those with religious fanaticism as zealots. For example, most people would probably consider the men who flew the airplanes into the World Trade Center as zealots. They believed so much in their cause that they were willing to give up their lives for the cause. Some people believe that the followers of Jim Jones who were willing to drink Kool-Aid laced with cyanide in a mass

FRAYER MODEL

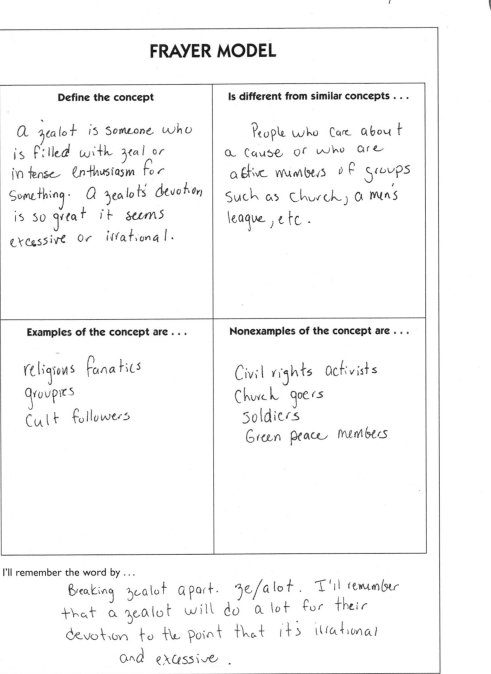

Define the concept	Is different from similar concepts . . .
A zealot is someone who is filled with zeal or intense enthusiasm for something. A zealots devotion is so great it seems excessive or irrational.	People who care about a cause or who are active members of groups such as church, a men's league, etc.

Examples of the concept are . . .	Nonexamples of the concept are . . .
religious fanatics groupies Cult followers	Civil rights activists Church goers Soldiers Green peace members

I'll remember the word by . . .

Breaking zealot apart. Ze/a lot. I'll remember that a zealot will do a lot for their devotion to the point that it's irrational and excessive.

suicide were religious zealots who were willing to die for the cause they believed in.

4. Just because someone believes deeply in something, it does not make that person a zealot. Someone who believes in working for

civil rights for others, who is devoted to his or her faith, who is an enthusiastic member of a club or group, or who supports a political cause would not be considered a zealot. Such people obviously are enthusiastic about their groups or causes but not to the point of abandoning all other human values.

5. Following are some examples and nonexamples of the word *zealot*. Discuss how you would classify these: a groupie for a band, a minister of a church, a soldier who willingly dies to save his platoon, a presidential candidate, and Yolanda Saldivar.

6. Create your own connections to the word *zealot* in order to help you commit the word to memory.

When and Why Would I Use the Frayer Model?

Due to the extensive time it takes to use the Frayer Model, you would probably only use this instructional model when introducing students to an umbrella concept that is extremely significant to a unit of study. After your initial teaching, you could return to the model several times throughout the unit. The example given here was connected to a novel being read in language arts class; however, the instructional strategy can be used in any content area. For example, if students in science were beginning their study of force and motion, the teacher might guide them through the Frayer Model with *force* and *motion* as the concepts. In this way, the teacher could assess students' prior knowledge of the concepts and add to that knowledge with attributes of the concepts.

Using science concepts as an example, students would first define the concepts in terms of their general knowledge of the words: forcing someone or something to act against its will or any movement. The teacher would give students the definition of how these words are used in science. The students and teacher would then discuss and note how force and motion are related to, but different from, gravity, free fall, acceleration, and velocity. In this way, the model helps facilitate the discussion of academic vocabulary that will be used in this unit of study. Students could then read their textbooks, *The Story of Science* (Hakim 2005), and *Fatal Forces* (Arnold 1999). After reading from these three sources, groups of students could create their own examples and nonexamples of the concepts of force and motion in science.

A modified version of this process, as shown in the graphic organizer, would provide students with guided practice in discovering and noting attributes and nonattributes or examples and nonexamples of words. Students' independence with the graphic will depend on the demonstrations the teacher provides.

Research/Origins/Further Reading

Arnold, N. 1999. *Fatal Forces*. New York: Scholastic.

Frayer, D. A., W. C. Frederick, and H. J. Klausmeier. 1969. *A Schema for Testing the Level of Concept Mastery*. Technical Report No. 16. Madison: University of Wisconsin Research and Development Center for Cognitive Learning.

Hakim, J. 2005. *The Story of Science: Newton at the Center.* Washington and New York: Smithsonian Books.

Ryder, R. J., and M. F. Graves. 1994. *Reading and Learning in Content Areas*. New York: Macmillan College.

Yolen, J., and B. Coville. 1998. *Armageddon Summer*. New York: Harcourt Children's Books.

FREQUENT CONTACT

What Is Frequent Contact?

Research has shown that effective vocabulary instruction supports in-depth processing of words. Frequent Contact provides students with an opportunity to think about, discuss, categorize, and use words based on inferences students make about a variety of clustered words. Given a list of words, students are asked to determine who or what would have the most *frequent contact* (Jantzen 1985) with each word.

How Does Frequent Contact Work?

When using Frequent Contact as an instructional strategy to foster deep processing of vocabulary words, the following steps are followed:

1. Students are given a list of words and three category labels.
2. Students draw three columns on a page and put one label at the top of each column.
3. Students work in pairs or small groups to read, think about, and discuss each of the words and decide who or what (category label) would have the most frequent contact with each of the words in the list.
4. Students place each of the words in the list under one or more of the category labels based on frequency of contact between word and label.
5. If students can justify putting a word in more than one category, they should place the words in all categories that make sense.
6. Members of one group make their completed categories known for the rest of the class.
7. Students then discuss differences in their categories from the posted list.
8. Answers are "right" if students can justify placing a word in a category.
9. Following discussion, students use one of the clusters of words to support their writing.

When and Why Would I Use This Instructional Strategy?

This instructional strategy would be used when you want students to examine and discriminate between roles and activities of a person or object. In Example 1, an English teacher is using Frequent Contact following students' reading of *Monster* (Myers 1999). Students are given three category labels: defendant, prosecution, and defense. They are asked to put each of the words in a category (or more than one, if applicable) based on who (defendant, prosecution, or defense) would have the most *frequent contact* with the word in the list. For example, students would look at the word *Bible* in their list of words and determine that the defendant would have the most frequent contact with that word as he has to swear his honesty in court by using the Bible.

FREQUENT CONTACT
Monster

Read and discuss each of the words in the word bank. As you discuss the words, decide which column each should be placed in based on which words would have the most frequent contact with each category's label. If you can justify placing words in more than on category, you should do that. When you finish, circle those words that ended up in more than one category.

Defendant	Prosecution	Defense

testimony	judge	restraints	subpoena
witnesses	alibi	remarks	affidavit
deposition	crime scene	expert testimony	news reporter
warden	past precedents	ruling	verdict
Bible	cell	guard	jury

Use the words in one of your columns to make a case for Steve's guilt or innocence.

Adapted from S. Jantzen. 1985. Scholastic Composition, Level 2. *New York: Scholastic.*

Example 1

In this way, the teacher and her students are able to explore the roles, responsibilities, and characteristics of the major characters in the novel. In addition, many students would have heard some or all of the words in the list but most students would need to determine specific definitions for some words that are familiar but not known prior to categorizing the words. While *Bible* makes more sense in the Defendant category, other words could logically be place in all three categories. Students would likely place words such as verdict, witnesses, and testimony in two or three of the categories. The only parameter is that students be able to defend the placement of words in a given category. When students have finished categorizing the words, they use the words in any one of the columns to defend or denounce Steve's innocence from the point of view of the defendant, the prosecution, or the defense. Each category of words then becomes a word bank that supports students' writing.

This activity can be adapted for most topics covered in content classrooms. For example, in science, during a study of the brain, the teacher might have the following headings: premotor cortex, amygdala, and posterior cingulate. Students would then use lists of words related to activities of and types of memory stored in each section of the brain. In algebra, category headings could include: x-intercept, y-intercept, and slope to explore words and functions related to graphing. In Example 2, Frequent Contact: Math Minds! students are using the activity to review and apply terms from three units of study in math: fractions, equations, and ratios and proportions. Regardless of the categories and words chosen, the goal of Frequent Contact is always the same: students are supported in discussing words and making inferences about words connected to a text or unit of study. They then use the words in the newly created word banks to demonstrate learning.

Research/Origins/Further Reading

Jantzen, S. 1985. *Scholastic Composition*, Level 2. New York: Scholastic.

Myers, W. D. 1999. *Monster*. New York: HarperCollins.

Nagy, W. E. 1988. *Teaching Vocabulary to Improve Reading Comprehension*. Urbana, IL: National Council Teachers of English; Newark, DE: International Reading Association.

FREQUENT CONTACT
MATH MINDS!

Read and discuss each of the words in the word bank. As you discuss the words, decide which column each should be placed in based on which words would have the most frequent contact with each category's label. If you can justify placing words in more than one category, you should do that. When you finish, circle those words that ended up in more than one category.

Fractions	Equations	Ratios and Proportions

whole numbers	comparison	denominator
solve	probability	simplify
linear	unknown	division
corresponding sides	similarity	common
variable	cross-multiplication	sum
one-step	mixed numbers	decimals
geometric relationships	two-step	quotient
expression	equivalent decimal	translating
least common	cross products	
substitute	corresponding angles	
algebraic	equals	
product	numerator	
scale-drawing	multiplication	

Work with others in your thinking/learning group to create a real-life problem where you would use fractions, equations, or ratios/proportions to solve the problem. For example, you might create a scenario where a photographer had to use rations/proportions to get a perfect picture. Or, you might be working as a stats person for your football team and need to use equations to show your team's overall losses for a game. Then, use words, algebra and/or arithmetic to show a solution for the problem. Use words (labels), steps, and diagrams to illustrate the solution. Finally, explain the solution to your problem using the key words you placed in the column that matches your problem. You won't need to use all the words but you should use those words that fit your problem and solution.

continued on next page

Example 2

Inside Words

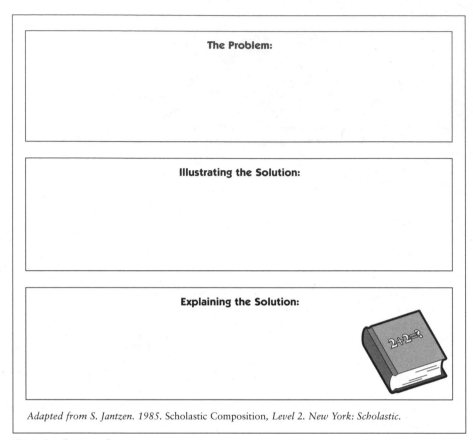

The Problem:

Illustrating the Solution:

Explaining the Solution:

Adapted from S. Jantzen. 1985. Scholastic Composition, Level 2. New York: Scholastic.

Example 2 (continued)

"I'M THINKING OF A WORD . . ."

What Is the "I'm Thinking of a Word . . ." Activity?

In *Words Count: Effective Vocabulary Instruction in Action*, Scott Greenwood has a chapter titled, "Vocabulary Lite." This chapter highlights activities that can be used to review and sustain interest in words through the use of games and highly engaging vocabulary activities. "I'm Thinking of a Word . . ." could be classified as a vocabulary lite activity. It is based on many games we've all played where someone thinks of a word and others have to guess what it is based on clues. In this activity, the teacher begins by saying he is thinking of a word and then giving clues to the word or concept until students can name the word and define it.

How Does the Activity Work?

The teacher chooses words taught during a recent novel or unit, taken from the classroom word wall, or relating to content-specific terms. The activity begins when the teacher says, "I'm thinking of a word . . ." The teacher completes this thought by providing students with a context, such as "I'm thinking of a word that we discussed in our study of colonial events in America." Or, "I'm thinking of a word that we use often in math class."

He allows a few wild guesses and then moves forward by giving students an example and a nonexample and continuing to repeat each previous clue. "I'm thinking of a word we discussed in our study of _____. An example of this word is _____. A nonexample of this word is _____." At this point, students will probably have several guesses. If they have guessed the word and can explain or describe the word's meaning in the context the teacher has created, then the teacher moves on to a new word and begins the game again. For example, students would have to explain the word's meaning in the context of colonial events in America or math class.

If students still have not guessed the word, the teacher would provide a richer, more detailed context by saying, "This word would always or usually be found in/connected to/used to . . ." and "This word would never be found in/connected to/used to . . ." By this time, students will have narrowed the possibilities and should be able to name and define the word.

When and Why Would I Use "I'm Thinking of a Word . . ."?

"I'm Thinking of a Word . . ." would usually be used as a review of words. This review could occur at the end of a unit so students could

---

"I'M THINKING OF A WORD . . ."

"I'm thinking of a word that . . ."

Examples of the word are . . .

Nonexamples of the word are . . .

Any ideas?

This word would always/usually . . .

This word would never . . .

The word is and it means . . .

---

solidify their understandings of specialized vocabulary words used in the unit. Since the teacher adds increasing amounts of contextual support, it could also be used as guided practice for students after a strategy lesson has been taught, demonstrating how students could figure out unknown words using context clues. Finally, if the teacher has a word wall, this activity can be used to highlight and review words that are on the word wall. In this way, students are reminded of word wall words and will begin or continue to use them in their writing.

Research/Origins/Further Reading

Greenwood, S. C. 2004. *Words Count: Effective Vocabulary Instruction in Action*. Portsmouth, NH: Heinemann.

I SPY:
A WORD
SCAVENGER
HUNT

What Is the I Spy Activity?

I Spy is an activity designed to provide students with an opportunity to apply and discover applications of target vocabulary words in real-life contexts. In most cases, students see lists of vocabulary words in the context of their textbooks or other teaching resources. This activity is based on the belief that middle and high school students should have "deeper explorations with language" (Beck, McKeown, and Kucan 2002) and that children remember more information when they relate words to known information (Stahl 1999; Craig and Tulving 1975). Relating the new to the known in the study of vocabulary can be finding examples and nonexamples, applying the word to known contexts, and making personal connections to the word. I Spy fosters all these activities as students go on scavenger hunts to find examples of the words they have studied in contexts other than their texts.

How Does I Spy Work?

I Spy works the same way any scavenger hunt works. In scavenger hunts, participants usually receive a list of items and must find those items somewhere. I Spy is a word scavenger hunt; students are given a list of words and must find examples of the word somewhere. In the example provided here, the social studies teacher and her students are studying the Revolutionary War. In the middle of the unit, students go on a scavenger hunt to find examples of the unit vocabulary words: revolution, traitor, infiltrate, declaration, and independence.

1. Create a list of words that are specific to the text or unit of study.
2. Give students the list of words and explain that they are looking for *examples* of the word and not the actual word. It is a bonus if they find the actual word but you really want them to discover the word in action.
3. Students work in groups and document where they discovered the word.
4. If possible, they bring an *artifact* to show the word in a new context. For example, if they find a newspaper article about a revolution, students cut the article out and bring that as an artifact. If they find a photograph of a revolution, they bring the photograph (or a copy) as an artifact.
5. Individually, students write what *connection* the target word in a new context has to what they are studying in the unit on the American Revolution.
6. If you have a word wall, artifacts can be displayed under each of the target words as a visual reminder of the word, its meanings, and its applications.

I SPY: A WORD SCAVENGER HUNT

Word/Concept	Where Discovered?	Word Artifact	Definition/ Connection to Unit of Study
Revolution			
Traitor			
Infiltrate			
Declaration			
Independence			

When and Why Would I Use This Activity?

The first reason you might want to use this activity is that students find it enjoyable. In addition, it is an ideal way to see if students have developed an in-depth understanding of the word and its attributes.

Students often memorize definitions for words from a content textbook but actually do not see these words as living words. They see the word only in relation to the chapter or unit of study. This activity brings the words to life for students, one that would be characterized as a "beyond the classroom" activity by Beck, McKeown, and Kucan (2002).

Our example is from a social studies classroom, but the activity could be used in any content area. In math, students might be looking for examples of words such as intersection, graph, line, solution, application, and variables in their study of linear equations and functions. In health, students might go on a scavenger hunt for words such as *pyramid, malnutrition, deficiency, nutrients, balanced,* and *vitamins* in their study of eating habits. Regardless of which words are chosen for each content area, the goals remain consistent: students transfer their knowledge of content-specific words to a larger context and then make connections between the context they discovered and the unit of study in which they have been involved.

Research/Origins/Further Reading

Beck, I. L., M. G. McKeown, and L. Kucan. 2002. *Bringing Words to Life: Robust Vocabulary Instruction.* New York: Guilford Press.

Craik, F. I. M., and E. Tulving. 1975. "Depth of Processing and the Retention of Words in Episodic Memory." *Journal of Experimental Psychology: General* 104: 268–94.

Stahl, S. A. 1999. *Vocabulary Development: From Research to Practice.* Newton Upper Falls, MA: Brookline Books.

LEAD

What Is LEAD?

The LEAD vocabulary strategy provides a way for the teacher to assess students' prior knowledge related to an anticipated activity or unit of study. In addition, the activity provides students with an opportunity to participate in listing specialized words, engage in an experience activity in which they use the words, and participate in a discussion using the words. The instructional strategy has three steps:

L   *List* specialized or academic vocabulary words related to the topic.

EA   Provide students with an *experience activity* where they would use the specialized words highlighted.

D   *Discuss* the topic using the specialized vocabulary words as a way of focusing the discussion.

How Does It Work?

As with any instructional strategy, there can be many variations in how this activity works. In Example 1, the teacher has highlighted words related to King Arthur and the Knights of the Round Table in anticipation of reading several King Arthur legends. The specialized vocabulary related to King Arthur legends has been listed for students. Students are shown a video clip of an Arthurian legend and asked to discuss the video clip and any other previous experiences they have had with movies or texts related to King Arthur legends.

As students discuss the movie and the texts, they are asked to use the specialized words in the list as well as to add other topic-related words that are not listed. The teacher and students then participate in a discussion where the teacher and students use the specialized words in both the questions and answers. For example, the teacher might query, "Did anyone talk about damsels in distress?" A student responds, "We did. We said *Pretty Woman* was based on a damsel in distress and Richard Gere was the knight in shining armor." Discussion (questioning and answering) continues in this fashion ensuring that all words are encountered several times.

A variation of this could occur using your content textbook. For example, in an algebra class, the teacher could ask students to work in groups to examine words in the upcoming chapter of their text. They could list the words used in the sidebar of the text or in the chapter-based glossary as well as words in bold or obviously specialized words that are repeated in the title and headings. The group lists are then combined into a whole-class list of specialized vocabulary related to the algebra chapter. As Example 2 shows, students then work together to find examples of the words. After discussing the words and their examples, they create questions for the whole class using the specialized words.

LEAD
EXPERIENCE-BASED VOCABULARY INSTRUCTION

L = Listing   EA = Experience Activity   D = Discussion

List

chivalry	pledge	betrayal
courtly	tournament	custom
knight	distress	code
jousting	dubbed	oath
damsel	rivalry	
heroic	skirmish	

Experience Activity

Work with members of your learning group and discuss what you know about King Arthur and the Knights of the Round Table. Use the words listed in the box above to describe what you know. Have you seen a movie about King Arthur and the Knights of the Round Table? If so, you probably know some other, related words. If anyone uses words related to King Arthur and the Knights during your discussion, write those words here.

Discussion

Did anyone know and talk about damsels in distress?
What did you think the words code and chivalry had to do with knights and knighthood?
Can you explain those words using any of the "knightly words" above?
I'm wondering if any of this is applicable today. What do you think?

Adapted from J. P. Klesius and S. E. Klesius (1989) and from J. M. Jacobson (1998)

Example 1

In the third example, a social studies teacher has asked students to watch the excerpts from the movie *Four Little Girls* (Lee 2001). Prior to watching the film, the teacher has read each of the words in the list and given students the opportunity to ask questions about any of the words. After watching the film, students work in groups to discuss their

LEAD
EXPERIENCE-BASED VOCABULARY INSTRUCTION

L = Listing   EA = Experience Activity   D = Discussion

List

plot points	linear	solution	x-intercept
coordinates	equation	interpret	y-intercept
intersection	variables	application	line
graph	ordered pair	coordinate plane	slope

Experience Activity

Work in pairs or groups to find examples of the words in the list in our classroom. You can use books, manipulatives, charts, or any other resources in the room or that you can see from the classroom windows. You can even create or build something that illustrates the meaning of the words. Discuss your findings and create a list of questions you will ask other groups. Make sure you use the words in our list in your questions.

Discussion

Teacher question: "Was anyone able to find a graph that showed a point of intersection?"
A student responds using the vocabulary word in his/her response and then follows his/her response with a new question.

Adapted from J. P. Klesius and S. E. Klesius (1989) and from J. M. Jacobson (1998)

Example 2

background knowledge of the Civil Rights Movement and their learning from the film. During their discussion, they are asked to use words from their word list in their comments and questions. When they finish, they

LEAD
EXPERIENCE-BASED VOCABULARY INSTRUCTION

L = Listing   EA = Experience Activity   D = Discussion

List

tolerance	dynamite	bigots
customs	overcome	inequality
Birmingham	states' rights	integration
nonviolence	racism	MLK, Jr.
segregation	boycott	
protest	discrimination	

Experience Activity

Watch the vido clip of Spike Lee's *Four Little Girls*. Using this video as the basis for your group's conversation, discuss what you know about the Civil Rights Movement. Try to use the words highlighted in the word list above for your comments and questions. At the end of your discussion, list other civil rights–related words that are not on the list.

Discussion

Now that we have read "Some Brave Children Meet a Roaring Bull" from *A History of US* (Hakim 1999), let's connect your discussion of the Civil Rights Movement to the new information we have. How is discrimination seen in the history book and the video? In what ways did movements embracing violence and movements supporting nonviolence work together? Or, were these two movements counterproductive?

Adapted from J. P. Klesius and S. E. Klesius (1989) and from J. M. Jacobson (1998)

Example 3

write down any additional civil rights–related words. The teacher brings the class back together for a discussion and frames each of her questions using words from the word list.

When and Why Would I Use This Strategy?

This strategy would be used to encourage students' active involvement in creating the specialized word list for any portion of the text you are using to teach concepts or content. The activity requires students to locate, examine, categorize, think critically, make applications, discuss, and question by using these words. It is an excellent way to anticipate both the specialized vocabulary and the content of your lesson. The student-generated questions can be revisited after reading the text to revise questions and answers to match new learning.

Research/Origins/Further Reading

Hakim, J. 1999. "Some Brave Children Meet a Roaring Bull." In *A History of US: All the People, 1945–1999*. New York: Oxford University Press.

Jacobson, J. M. 1998. *Content Area Reading: Integration with the Language Arts*. Albany, NY: Delmar.

Klesius. J. P., and S. E. Klesius. 1989. "Vocabulary on the Playground." *Reading Horizons* 29: 197–204.

Lee, S. 2001. *Four Little Girls*. HBO Production Video.

LIST-GROUP-LABEL

What Is List-Group-Label?

List-Group-Label (Taba 1967) is a brainstorming and categorizing activity that provides students with the opportunity to think about, discuss, categorize, and label words related to a central concept. Word knowledge is linked to the degree of background knowledge (Marzano 2004). Words that students generate in the process of this activity can serve as an excellent assessment tool for teachers in determining the degree of background knowledge students bring to the study.

How Does It Work?

As the name indicates, List-Group-Label asks students to follow three basic steps in completing the activity. Prior to beginning a book or unit of study, the teacher chooses a central concept or theme. Students are given the concept or theme word and asked to participate in the following activities:

1. **List**—Each student brainstorms words related to the word given by the teacher. I usually ask that students list as many words as they can but tell them they should list at least seven words. While some don't manage to list seven words, it motivates all students to list as many as possible. In the example shown here, Christine Landaker has given her students the word *war* and asked students to work independently to brainstorm words they think of when they hear this term.

2. **Group**—When each student completes the brainstorming part of this activity (List), students then work in small groups to share and combine their words into logical categories. As students attempt to combine three to five individual word lists, they begin to discover patterns of words. In this process, they are refining their knowledge of the concept. Students have to work together to combine their individual lists into a common group list that encompasses all of their words. One group's combined word list is shown in Example 1. As shown in this sample, students are eliminating words from their combined list as they begin to categorize them.

3. **Label**—Once students create their categories, they label each of them. These categories can become the basis for beginning a word wall for the unit or for students' portable word walls. The group in Example 2 created the following categories and labels: action words related to war; emotional words related to war; people who are involved in war; and, places/countries they associate with war.

As students worked through this activity, Christine was able to assess their background knowledge prior to beginning their unit of study.

LIST-GROUP-LABEL: WAR

SOLDIERS   ASSASSINATION
~~GENERAL~~   NUCLEAR WEAPONS
BLOOD   SPIES
GUNS   VIOLENCE
~~GUN POWDER~~   MARINES
~~UNIFORMS~~   BIN LADEN
~~CAMP~~   SADNESS
~~TANKS~~   GORY
~~SUBRINE~~   INTERNATIONAL AFFAIRS
AIRPLANES JETS
~~CARGO~~
DEATH
√ FIGHT
√ COUNTRIES
KILL
BAD
BOMBING
SCARED
POLITICANS
RUNNING
DESTROY
SHOOTING
SARGENT
AFGHANISTAN
HORSES
HOUSES BURING
HATERED
PESTILENCE
WAR BANDS
ARMIES

Example 1

Students could repeat this activity at the end of the unit on war and compare their post-study List-Group-Label with their pre-study list. Words representing all the group lists became part of the class word wall (Allen and Landaker 2005, 19–20).

ACTION WORDS
1. Fight
2. guns
~~3. jets~~
~~BOMBING~~
~~RUNNING~~
3. destroy
4. shooting
5. NUCLEAR WEAPONS
6. VIOLENCE
7. gory
8. Scared

EMOTIONAL WORDS
1. death
2. Kill
3. Bad
~~Scared~~
4. Blood
~~HOUSES BURNING~~
5. hatered
6. ASSASSINATION
7. Sadness
8. pestilence

People Who Are Involved
1. Soldiers
2. Politician
3. Sargent
4. WAR BANDS
5. ARMIES
6. Spies
7. MARINES
8. BIN LADEN
~~horses~~

PLACES & COUNTRIES
1. Afghanistan
2. horses
3. RUNNING
4. JETS
5. BOMBING
6. INTERNATIONAL AFFAIRS
7. HOUSES BURNING

Example 2

When and Why Would I Use This Strategy?

The brainstorming and categorizing of List-Group-Label can be used prior to beginning a unit, as shown in the example from Christine Landaker's classroom. Teachers in any content area can use the same instructional strategy by generating a term or concept that will be the focus of study in the classroom. For example, an English teacher who is about to begin teaching *To Kill a Mockingbird* (Lee 1960) could begin the activity by giving students the word *injustice* to begin List-Group-Label. A science teacher beginning a unit on the solar system would give students that term as the initial brainstorming word.

The products of this activity can be applied throughout the course of the unit as students use words from their lists when related words and concepts are encountered. I extend this activity by asking students to use their words and categories to generate questions or prediction statements related to what they think they will learn in this unit. These statements and questions can be revisited during and after the unit.

Research/Origins/Further Reading

Allen, J. 1999. *Words, Words, Words: Teaching Vocabulary in Grades 4–12*. Portland, ME: Stenhouse.

Allen, J., and C. Landaker. 2005. *Reading History: A Practical Guide to Improving Literacy*. New York: Oxford University Press.

Daniels, H., and S. Zemelman. 2004. *Subjects Matter: Every Teacher's Guide to Content-Area Reading*. Portsmouth, NH: Heinemann.

Lee, H. 1960. *To Kill a Mockingbird*. New York: Warner Books.

Marzano, R. J. 2004. *Building Background Knowledge for Academic Achievement: What Works in Schools*. Alexandria, VA: Association for Supervision and Curriculum Development.

Taba, H. 1967. *Teacher's Handbook for Elementary Social Studies*. Reading, MA: Addison-Wesley.

POSSIBLE QUESTIONS

What Is the Possible Questions Strategy?

I designed Possible Questions based on two lines of research: the role of student-generated questions to support comprehension (Martin 1985; Anderson and Armbruster 1984; Frase and Schwartz 1975) and the role of prediction in anticipating content (see Possible Sentences [Moore and Arthur 1981]). Possible Questions asks students to use specialized academic vocabulary words from an upcoming text to predict possible questions they believe the text will answer. Students revisit their questions to answer or revise them.

How Does It Work?

Choose specialized, critical vocabulary from the text or unit students will be studying. Words should be significant in terms of role in understanding the text or unit. Group words into clusters of two or three that would logically go together in terms of information related to the topic of study. Ask students to work in groups to generate questions using the clustered words. The questions should be ones students believe will be answered in the course of their reading about the topic.

During and after reading, students use their questions to monitor and check for understanding. If one or more of their sentences were answered, students write answers to the questions in the space provided. If students need to revise their questions to create questions using the target words, they do so and then answer the questions. Finally, students use the target words to create a visual representation of what they have learned about the topic.

When and Why Would I Use This Strategy?

You would want to use this strategy to build background knowledge and anticipate content prior to beginning a chapter in the text, a new novel, or a unit of study. Research has shown that when students generate questions anticipating both the content of the text and questions they may be asked about the text (Palinscar and Brown 1985), comprehension improves. In addition, the student-generated questions provide you and your students with the opportunity to highlight the most significant content in what you have read.

In the first example shown here, students will be reading about viruses and bacteria in their science textbook and supplemental reading. The teacher is using specialized, topical vocabulary from the readings for Possible Questions. During and after reading, students use questions to monitor and check understanding of the content. They then apply what they have learned about the content and the vocabu-

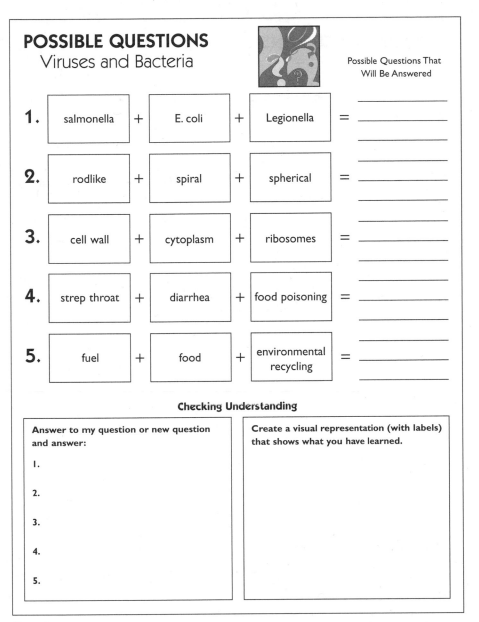

POSSIBLE QUESTIONS
Viruses and Bacteria

Possible Questions That
Will Be Answered

1. salmonella + E. coli + Legionella = _____
_____

2. rodlike + spiral + spherical = _____
_____

3. cell wall + cytoplasm + ribosomes = _____
_____

4. strep throat + diarrhea + food poisoning = _____
_____

5. fuel + food + environmental recycling = _____
_____

Checking Understanding

Answer to my question or new question and answer:

1.

2.

3.

4.

5.

Create a visual representation (with labels) that shows what you have learned.

Example 1

lary by creating a visual to demonstrate learning. The vocabulary words then become the labels for their visual.

In the second example, a social studies teacher is introducing students to examples of intolerance in the United States. Students have examined pictures and listened to lyrics to a song related to the Zoot

Inside Words

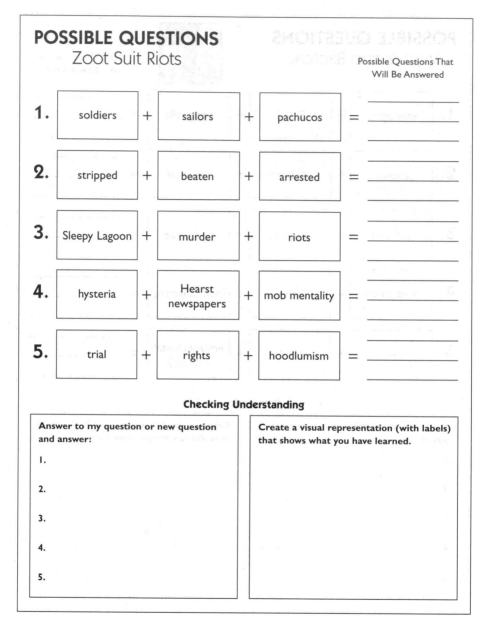

POSSIBLE QUESTIONS
Zoot Suit Riots

Possible Questions That
Will Be Answered

1. | soldiers | + | sailors | + | pachucos | = _____

2. | stripped | + | beaten | + | arrested | = _____

3. | Sleepy Lagoon | + | murder | + | riots | = _____

4. | hysteria | + | Hearst newspapers | + | mob mentality | = _____

5. | trial | + | rights | + | hoodlumism | = _____

Checking Understanding

Answer to my question or new question
and answer:

1.

2.

3.

4.

5.

Create a visual representation (with labels)
that shows what you have learned.

Example 2

Suit Riots prior to examining the words and creating their prediction
questions. Examples of student questions include:

- What caused the soldiers and sailors to go after the pachucos?
- Were the pachucos stripped, beaten, and arrested for causing the riots?

- Was there a murder at Sleepy Lagoon? Did the murder cause a riot?
- Did the Hearst newspapers try to stop the riots or did they help create hysteria and mob mentality?
- What is hoodlumism? Did the pachucos have any rights at the trial or were they just considered hoodlums who didn't deserve rights?

These examples show the effective use of Possible Questions in two areas of study but the instructional strategy could be used in any content area. Teachers generate lists of topic-specific vocabulary words; provide students with some background knowledge; and give them the opportunity to use that background knowledge and the vocabulary words to help them predict questions they hope to get answered during the unit of study.

Research/Origins/Further Reading

Anderson, T. H., and B. B. Armbruster. 1984. "Studying." In *Handbook of Reading Research*, ed. P. D. Pearson, 657–79. New York: Longman.

Frase, L. T., and B. J. Schwartz. 1975. "Effect of Question Production and Answering on Prose Recall." *Journal of Educational Psychology* 67: 628–35.

Martin, M. A. 1985. "Students' Applications of Self-Questioning Study Techniques: An Investigation of Their Efficiency." *Reading Psychology* 6: 69–83.

Moore, D. W., and S. V. Arthur. 1981. "Possible Sentences." In *Reading in the Content Areas: Improving Classroom Instruction*, eds. E. K. Dishner, T. W. Bean, and J. E. Readence, 138–43. Dubuque, IA: Kendall/Hunt.

Palinscar, A. S., and A. L. Brown. 1985. "Reciprocal Teaching Activities to Promote Reading with Your Mind." In *Reading, Thinking, and Concept Development: Interactive Strategies for the Class*, ed. E. J. Cooper. New York: The College Board.

POSSIBLE
SENTENCES

What Is the Possible Sentences Strategy?

Possible Sentences (Moore and Arthur 1981; Moore and Moore 1992) is a prereading strategy that gives students the opportunity to predict the content of upcoming reading based on targeted vocabulary words. Students use two or more of the words in a sentence that they predict will occur in the upcoming text. It also serves as an activity that can help students monitor comprehension during reading and review content after reading. When students finish reading, they can use the text to confirm or revise their predicted sentences.

How Does It Work?

Possible Sentences is one of the best instructional activities I have seen for building background knowledge with targeted vocabulary words. Students enjoy the activity *and* read more carefully than they might otherwise because they are looking for their words and the accuracy of their sentences. Possible Sentences has the following steps:

1. Select words from the text that are critical to students' understanding of the reading. Choose some words that will be new to students and some words that are familiar to them. All words chosen should be significant in the text. I usually anticipate this activity with a read-aloud that builds context for the words they will encounter here. For example, prior to reading about early empires and the beginning of laws in World History, I might read "Prisons and Punishments" from *Oh, Yikes! History's Grossest, Wackiest Moments* (Masoff 2006). In this way, students have some background knowledge so their predicted sentences are more focused.

2. Read each of the targeted words aloud.

3. Assign student groups and ask students to write sentences they believe they will read in the text. They should use two or more words in each sentence but they should not use so many words that the sentence is hard to revise.

4. Students keep track of their predicted sentences and each group contributes one or more of their sentences when the teachers calls for volunteers to share sentences for whole-class charting.

5. If all words in the target list are not used in sentences generated by groups, create class-generated sentences for the remaining words. All words in the target list should be used.

6. Students use their sentences as support while reading the text. They mark each of their sentences as true, false, or unknown based on the accuracy of their content compared to the text. If the sentences are inaccurate in terms of the text's contents, they revise their sentences using the target words so their sentences accurately reflect the content.

POSSIBLE SENTENCES
Triangle Shirtwaist Fire

Key Vocabulary

sunny	workers	freight elevators
ten-story	locked	ablaze
Triangle Shirtwaist	women	floor
framed	Teletype	rules
oil	cloth	fire
stairways	windows	reform
fire escapes	message	never
warned	investigation	identified
	soaked	supervisors

Possible Sentences

1. Triangle Shirtwaist is a clothing store where women work.
2. The entrances to the fire escapes were locked so they jumped.
3. It was a rule that women could help other workers.
4. The stairways, fire escape, and windows were blocked.
5. No supervisors helped the workers.
6. The fire started from all the cloth on the floors.
7. Women were never to leave work early.
8. No message was sent that the building was ablaze.
9. There was an investigation.
10. It was a sunny day.

Using Sentences as a Guide/Modifying Predictions

Mark each of the possible sentences with True, False, or Unknown. When you finish reading, return to your sentences and see how you could modify them so they are accurate in terms of the content of the passage you have read.

1. Triangle Shirtwaist was a factory where shirtwaists were manufactured.
2. There were not enough fire escapes and the fire escapes collapsed from too many people.
3. It was a rule that doors were locked by the owners to prevent theft.
4. The stairways and fire escapes were blocked.
5. Supervisors got in the freight elevator and tried to escape without helping the workers.
6. The fire started from a spark (maybe cigarette) with cloth soaked by oil from the sewing machines.
7. We didn't read anything about this.
8. A message was sent by Teletype.
9. True.
10. True.

Example 1

When and Why Would I Use This Strategy?

The strategy is an ideal way to build background knowledge and generate student interest in a text. Having seen and worked with the targeted vocabulary words creates a natural curiosity about the

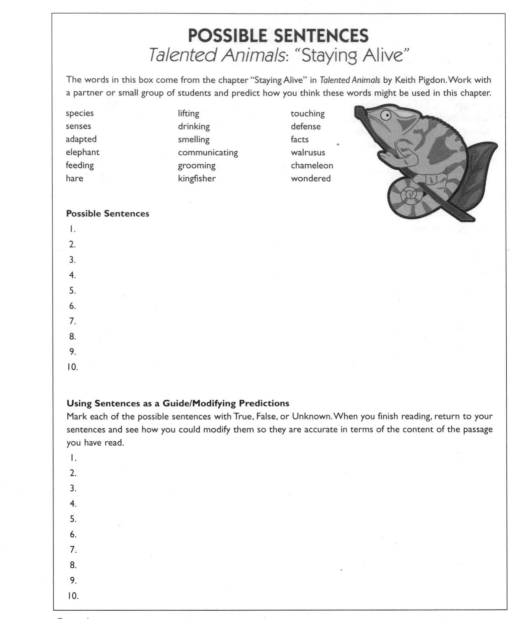

POSSIBLE SENTENCES
Talented Animals: "Staying Alive"

The words in this box come from the chapter "Staying Alive" in *Talented Animals* by Keith Pigdon. Work with a partner or small group of students and predict how you think these words might be used in this chapter.

species	lifting	touching
senses	drinking	defense
adapted	smelling	facts
elephant	communicating	walrusus
feeding	grooming	chameleon
hare	kingfisher	wondered

Possible Sentences

1.
2.
3.
4.
5.
6.
7.
8.
9.
10.

Using Sentences as a Guide/Modifying Predictions

Mark each of the possible sentences with True, False, or Unknown. When you finish reading, return to your sentences and see how you could modify them so they are accurate in terms of the content of the passage you have read.

1.
2.
3.
4.
5.
6.
7.
8.
9.
10.

Example 2

accuracy of their predictions. This interest sustains them throughout the reading of their text and serves as an excellent tool for synthesizing and summarizing the most significant information and ideas in what students have read.

There are two examples shown here: A high school social studies teacher has her students participating in a Possible Sentences activity prior to reading about the Triangle Shirtwaist Fire (Allen and Daley 2004) and an elementary teacher has her students participating in the activity prior to a shared reading of an Explorations book, *Talented Animals* (Pigdon 2006). The structure of the activity and its purpose remain the same regardless of students' ages and the complexity of the text.

Research/Origins/Further Reading

Allen, J., and P. Daley. 2004. *Scholastic Read Aloud Anthology*. New York: Scholastic Teaching Resources.

Masoff, J. 2006. *Oh, Yikes! History's Grossest, Wackiest Moments*. New York: Workman.

Moore, D. W., and S. V. Arthur. 1981. "Possible Sentences." In *Reading in the Content Areas: Improving Classroom Instruction*, eds. E. K. Dishner, T. W. Bean, and J. E. Readence, 138–42. Dubuque, IA: Kendall/Hunt.

Moore, S. A., and D. W. Moore. 1992. "Possible Sentences: An Update." In *Reading in the Content Areas: Improving Classroom Instruction*, 3rd ed., eds. E. K. Dishner, T. W. Bean, and J. E. Readence, 196–201. Dubuque, IA: Kendall/Hunt.

Pigdon, K. 2006. *Talented Animals*. San Marcos, CA: Okapi Educational Materials/Curtain Communications Pty.

PREVIEWING CONTENT VOCABULARY

What Is the Previewing Content Vocabulary Instructional Strategy?

Previewing Content Vocabulary is an instructional strategy based on Dale's (1965) research on what it means to know a word. Researchers agree that matching a word to a definition demonstrates surface-level knowledge of a word. Dale cited four levels of word knowledge:

1. I've never seen the word before.
2. I've heard the word, but I don't know what it means.

3. I recognize it in context and know that it is connected/related to
   _____ (words or concept).
4. I know the word and can use it appropriately.

Previewing Content Vocabulary is a way for teachers and students to assess students' background knowledge of the words and concepts they will encounter in a specific reading assignment or unit of study.

How Does It Work?

Use the graphic organizer for Previewing Content Vocabulary to guide your students through this activity. Read the title of the chapter or text to students and ask them to brainstorm words they think they will encounter in reading a text with this title. In the example shown here, a World History class is studying a textbook chapter entitled, "The New Kingdom: A Woman Pharaoh." After students brainstorm words they think they will encounter in reading this chapter, direct them to the word list at the bottom of the page. These words are taken from the text students will read. You can read the words to the students or ask students to work in groups and determine their level of knowledge of each of the content words they will encounter in reading the upcoming chapter or text. Students list each word in the appropriate category based on their prior knowledge of the word. Words in the third and fourth quadrants (students know definitions, connections, and uses) can be explored in the context of reading and discussion. Words that most students classify as unknown (never having seen or heard the word) should be words focused on for preteaching prior to students' reading of the text.

When and Why Would I Use This Strategy?

This strategy would be used to assess your students' knowledge of the words and concepts in a specific text. In the course of students

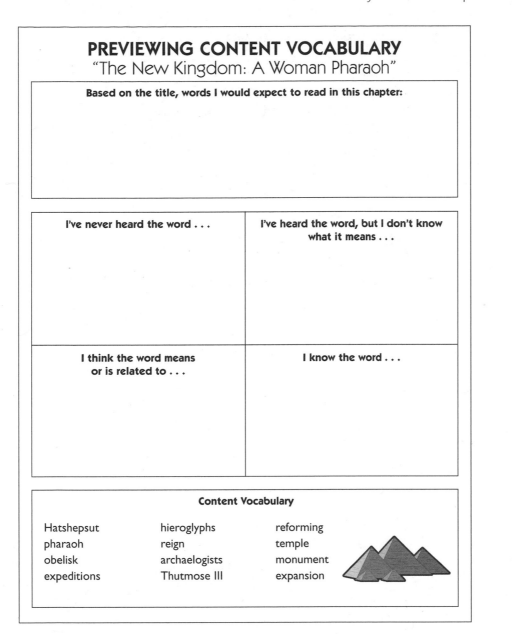

PREVIEWING CONTENT VOCABULARY
"The New Kingdom: A Woman Pharaoh"

Based on the title, words I would expect to read in this chapter:

I've never heard the word . . .	I've heard the word, but I don't know what it means . . .
I think the word means or is related to . . .	I know the word . . .

Content Vocabulary

Hatshepsut	hieroglyphs	reforming
pharaoh	reign	temple
obelisk	archaelogists	monument
expeditions	Thutmose III	expansion

reading, discussing, and categorizing the words based on their level of knowledge, you are able to ascertain not only their level of word knowledge, but also their general background knowledge for the events or concepts you are about to study with them. With limited time to devote to word study, this activity can help you choose the least-known words for preteaching.

Research/Origins/Further Reading

Dale, E. 1965. "Vocabulary Measurement: Techniques and Major Findings." *Elementary English* 42: 82–88.

Beck, I. L., M. G. McKeown, and R. C. Omanson. 1987. "The Effects and Uses of Diverse Vocabulary Instructional Techniques." In *The Nature of Vocabulary Acquisition*, eds. M. G. McKeown and M. E. Curtis, 147–63. Hillsdale, NJ: Erlbaum.

SEMANTIC FEATURE ANALYSIS

What Is a Semantic Feature Analysis?

A Semantic Feature Analysis (Johnson and Pearson 1984) provides a format for students to think about, discuss, and determine the critical attributes of related words. Each horizontal row in a Semantic Feature Analysis lists one of the words from the cluster of related words. Each vertical column lists one semantic feature that some of the words share. All words in the rows will not share all words in the columns; one purpose of the Semantic Feature Analysis is to provide students with an opportunity to determine the differences between words that share some common characteristics.

How Does a
Semantic Feature Analysis Work?

When creating a Semantic Feature Analysis for your students, choose a group of words that share some common characteristics. For example, you might choose several characters from a novel. These characters would be listed down the left-hand side of a grid (horizontal rows). Choose characteristics each might possess and list those characteristics across the top (vertical columns). Students discuss each character, placing a + (plus sign) in the box under the columns for all characteristics that apply to that character. They place a – (minus sign) in the column if the character doesn't exhibit the characteristic. If students are unsure of whether the character has or has exhibited the characteristic, they would place a ? (question mark) in the column.

The Semantic Feature Analysis is effective with any cluster of related words and their characteristics: types of trees, musical instruments, species of birds, geometric shapes, branches of government, political parties, war, and so on. In every case, the grid is created in the same way.

When and Why Would I Use
a Semantic Feature Analysis?

A feature analysis is an ideal instructional strategy when you are teaching a unit where students need to discriminate between items that have some common characteristics. In the first example shown here, the teacher is teaching a unit on letter writing and is using a Semantic Feature Analysis so students learn the distinguishing characteristics of each type of letter. Students generate all the headings that are in the vertical columns from the examples the teacher provides and the teacher provides the technical terms (salutation, heading, etc.) if students do not know the name for the feature. Students then have a self-assessment tool to use as they write letters to make sure they have included conventional features for the type of letter being written.

SEMANTIC FEATURE ANALYSIS
Comparison: Attributes of Letters

	Diary Journal	Friendly Letter	Editorial Letter	Business Letter
Date				
Information				
Inside Address				
Heading				
Salutation (Greeting)				
Closing				
Organization				
P.S.				
Language (formal/ informal)				
Paragraphs (Body)				
Enclosure				
Attention Line				
Subject Line				

Example 1

The second example shown here is a Semantic Feature Analysis used by a history teacher. In this case, the teacher wants students to think about and discuss the different names used for heads of government or rulers. Types of rulers are listed down the left-hand side of the grid (horizontal rows): queen/king, tsar, emperor/empress, president.

SEMANTIC FEATURE ANALYSIS
Characteristics of Rulers

	Queen	King	Tsar	Emperor/ Empress	President
elected					
complete power					
unlimited authority					
leader					
tyrant					
appointed					
chief executive					
royalty					
Commander in Chief					
sovereign					
ruler					
monarch					

Example 2

Some characteristics of rulers are listed across the top (vertical columns): elected, complete power, unlimited authority, and so forth. Students can take each ruler and determine whether the characteristic applies to the ruler. When this is completed, students can then use their Semantic Feature Analysis to compare and contrast types of rulers/leaders.

Research/Origins/Further Reading

Anders, P., and C. Box. 1986. "Semantic Feature Analysis: An Interactive Strategy for Vocabulary Development and Text Comprehension." *Journal of Reading* 29 (7): 610–16.

Johnson, D. D., and P. D. Pearson. 1984. *Teaching Reading Vocabulary*. 2nd ed. New York: Holt, Rinehart and Winston.

Pittelman, S. D., J. E. Heimlich, R. L. Berglund, and M. P. French. 1991. *Semantic Feature Analysis: Classroom Applications*. Newark, DE: International Reading Association.

SEMANTIC MAPPING

What Is Semantic Mapping?

Semantic Mapping (Heimlich and Pittelman 1986) is a teacher-directed study of a word or concept in relation to other related words and ideas. The teacher begins a Semantic Mapping activity by providing a word or concept about to be studied and students brainstorm characteristics, attributes, related words and ideas, and specific examples of the word. The map is a graphic representation of this thinking and discussion. Discussion is a significant aspect of a Semantic Mapping activity (Stahl and Clark 1987). In addition, there is a significant line of research that supports the positive impact of Semantic Mapping in terms of students' memory of the targeted word and recognition of that word in a variety of contexts (Johnson, Toms-Bronowski, and Pittelman 1982).

How Does It Work?

Semantic Mapping works with any word, concept, phrase, event, character, or theme. It begins with the teacher providing the word that students will be exploring. In the first example shown, Christine Landaker and the students in her middle school classroom are exploring the Civil War prior to their reading and study. They brainstormed predicted categories they would learn about in their study: people, places, causes/events, other related information. They then worked in groups to come up with details they already knew prior to their reading and study.

Once this information was gathered, students drew the group semantic map in their individual academic journals. Academic journals

Example 1

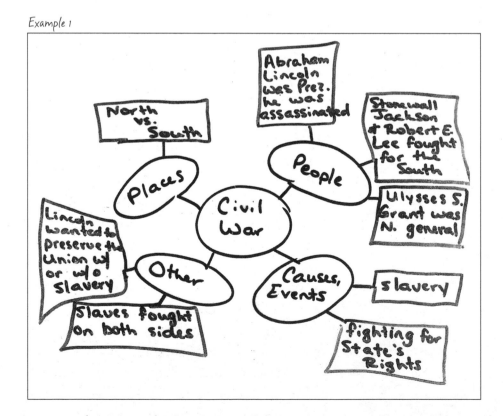

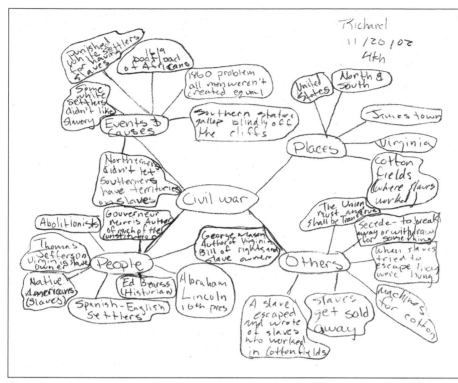

Richard
11/20/02
4th

Punished while settlers for having slaves

Dockload of Africans

1860 problem all men weren't created equal

United States

North & South

Some white settlers didn't like slavery

Events & Causes

Southern states gallop blindly off the cliffs

Places

Jamestown

Virginia

Cotton fields (where slaves worked)

Northerners didn't let Southerners have territories or slaves

Civil war

The Union must and shall be preserved

Secede- to break away or withdraw for something

Gouverneur Morris Author of much of the Constitution

Abolitionists

George Mason Author of Virginia Bill of rights and slave owner

Others

When slaves tried to escape they were hung

Thomas Jefferson Virginia owned a slave

People

Native Americans (Slaves)

Ed Bearss (Historian)

Abraham Lincoln 16th pres

A slave escaped and wrote of slaves who worked in cotton fields

Slaves get sold away

Machines for cotton

Spanish-English Settlers

Example 2

are individual notebooks kept by each student and used as a natural part of each class as well as support during assessments. Teachers vary in the sections they ask students to keep in their academic journals but typical sections include note taking, language collection (vocabulary), and strategies learned (how-to lessons). During their study of this event, Christine gave students opportunities to add to their semantic maps as they discovered additional information. The semantic map in Example 2 shows one student's note taking using his semantic map. The map then serves as a review and study tool as well as an organized way to highlight significant aspects of their study.

When and Why Would I Use This Strategy?

This activity lends itself to use at any stage in your study of a concept, event, theme, or unit of study. It provides an assessment for you about the background knowledge your students bring to the study and gives students in the class an overview of critical aspects of the study you will be doing. During your study, it becomes a place for students to take notes and organize the notes in a meaningful way. Students might choose to redo their semantic maps once they have gathered enough information that a new map and its design might better help them keep track of their learning. Finally, it serves as a way for you and your students to review their knowledge base prior to any academic writing or demonstrations of learning you might ask students to do.

Research/Origins/Further Reading

Heimlich, J. E., and S. D. Pittelman. 1986. *Semantic Mapping: Classroom Applications*. Newark, DE: International Reading Association.

Johnson, D. D., S. Toms-Bronowski, and S. D. Pittelman. 1982. *An Investigation of the Effectiveness of Semantic Mapping and Semantic Feature Analysis with Intermediate Grade Children*. Program Report 83-3. Madison: Wisconsin Center for Educational Research, University of Wisconsin.

Stahl, S. A., and C. H. Clark. 1987. "The Effects of Participatory Expectations in Classroom Discussion on the Learning of Science Vocabulary." *American Educational Research Journal* 24: 541–56.

SURVIVAL
OF THE FITTEST

What Is the Survival of the Fittest Activity?

In Survival of the Fittest, students are asked to determine which word couldn't survive with the others in a given list. Survival of the Fittest can be used as a review of content vocabulary related to a topic or unit of study. The activity is based on three strands of research that connect effective vocabulary instruction to increased learning: Students need multiple exposures to the word (Stahl and Fairbanks 1986); exposures should be in varied contexts (McKeown, et al. 1985); and instruction should establish connections among instructed items (Nagy 1988).

How Does It Work?

Survival of the Fittest works with predetermined groups of words related to the topic or unit of study. Students are given clusters of four or five words and asked to determine which word would not survive or doesn't fit with the others. Students eliminate that word and create a label that would be appropriate for the remaining words. The label should describe what makes the remaining words fits together. An additional task could include asking students to generate a new word that would take the place of the eliminated word so that it would fit with the remaining words.

When and Why Would I Use This Strategy?

Survival of the Fittest is an effective activity for students to review technical vocabulary related to a topic or unit of study. If used as a review, students will have had multiple exposures to the words and to other students' knowledge of the words prior to application in an assessment or evaluation. The activity can be used as an assessment tool for individuals or small groups or used as a review prior to an evaluation of content knowledge.

Examples of Survival of the Fittest word clusters follow:

1. _____	2. _____
Salmonella	dictator
E. coli	despot
Legionella	president
Shigella	autocrat
Measles	tyrant

Research/Origins/Further Reading

Alvermann, D. E., and S. E. Phelps. 1994. *Content Reading and Literacy: Succeeding in Today's Diverse Classrooms*. Boston: Allyn and Bacon.

SURVIVAL OF THE FITTEST

Read and discuss the words in each of the clusters of words. Determine which word does not fit with the other words in each cluster. Eliminate that word and then create a label that would include the words that are left in the cluster of words. For a challenge, generate a new word that would replace the eliminated word *and* fit with the remaining words in the cluster.

1._____

Legionella

chicken pox

salmonella

E. coli

shigella

McKeown, M., I. Beck, R. Omanson, and M. Pople. 1985. "Some Effects of the Nature and Frequency of Vocabulary Instruction on the Knowledge and Use of Words." *Reading Research Quarterly* 20: 522–35.

Nagy, W. E. 1988. *Teaching Vocabulary to Improve Reading Comprehension*. Urbana, IL: National Council Teachers of English; Newark, DE: International Reading Association.

Stahl, S., and M. Fairbanks. 1986. "The Effects of Vocabulary Instruction: A Model-Based Meta-Analysis." *Review of Educational Research* 56: 72–110.

THINK-PAIR-SHARE: COLLABORATE FOR UNDERSTANDING

What Is Think-Pair-Share?

Think-Pair-Share: Collaborate for Understanding is based on the collaborative learning structure Think-Pair-Share developed by Frank Lyman (1981). Think-Pair-Share describes three stages for students' active learning. In the first stage, a learner works independently to *think* about a question/issue; in the second stage, the learner *pairs* with another learner to share ideas; in the final stage, two pairs of students work together to collaborate and *share* their ideas. In the vocabulary activity using this structure, students participate in those same action stages with a target vocabulary word.

How Does It Work?

Using this active learning structure in any classroom has the advantage of providing students with opportunities to think and note their initial understanding of a word. The concept or word is targeted in context. For example, if a health teacher is about to begin a unit of learning focused on digestion, the day's lesson could focus on molecules and nutrients. The teacher would begin by presenting the target word(s) in context by reading from *Food Rules!* (Haduch 2001):

> *Molecules are the only things that your body can really use. That's what digestion is all about—making a slush of molecules that your body can use for energy and for growth and repair.*
>
> *Now, here's the real action part. The molecules, now called nutrients, are so tiny that they can pass through the walls of your small intestine and into your blood vessels. (9)*

After the teacher reads this portion of text, each student takes time to think about what molecules and nutrients are and notes his or her thoughts about the words' meanings. After students have had time to note their thoughts, the teacher gives students the opportunity to collaborate with another student. Each student describes, explains, or compares individual definitions of the words. At this point, the teacher can continue the Think-Pair-Share process or provide an additional reading experience so students have more information about the words. Whether the teacher provides additional information or not, students then move to the final stage in this process.

Each pair of students then combines with another pair of students to share their understanding of the words and how these words are connected to digestion. Students are now in groups of four and each group will share their definitions for the words. In this activity, I ask groups to create a visual or dramatize their understanding of the words as a way of sharing that information with other students.

When and Why Would I Use This Strategy?

Think-Pair-Share: Collaborate for Understanding can be used before beginning a unit or text so you and your students can assess their prior knowledge of the vocabulary words critical to their understanding of the themes and concepts in the unit. It can be used frequently throughout the unit in order to introduce students to new words as encountered and to give students the opportunity to discuss their understanding of the words they are encountering. It can be used at the end of the unit by asking students to work in groups, with each group taking one or two of the academic words in the unit and preparing visuals or presentations that review and demonstrate their understanding of the academic vocabulary used in the course of study. As a teacher, you are able to assess students' understanding of words and concepts before, during, and after any unit of study.

Think-Pair-Share as a collaborative learning structure has many advantages:

- It provides students with think time prior to discussion.
- It allows for independent and collaborative learning.
- It gives students opportunities to collaborate to refine definitions.
- It invites more equal participation as all students share with one other and then with another pair of students.
- It engages students in active learning.
- It invites students to share their understanding in kinesthetic and visual modes.

Research/Origins/Further Reading/

Haduch, B. 2001. *Food Rules!* New York: Dutton Children's Books.
Lyman, F. 1981. "The Responsive Classroom Discussion." In
    Mainstreaming Digest, ed. A. S. Anderson. College Park:
    University of Maryland College of Education.

VOCAB-O-GRAM

What Is a Vocab-o-Gram?

A Vocab-o-Gram (Blachowicz 1986) is a graphic organizer that gives students the opportunity to make predictions about a story using words from the story with categories of a story structure. The Vocab-o-Gram provides students with a list of vocabulary words from the story to be read. The graphic organizer contains elements of story structure: setting, characters, conflict, plot, resolution. Students use the vocabulary words to make predictions about each of the elements of story structure.

How Does the Vocab-o-Gram Work?

The teacher selects vocabulary words from a story students are going to read. A graphic organizer is created with elements of story structure provided as categories or questions. Typical elements of story structure include setting, characters, conflict, plot, and resolution. Depending on your instructional goals, other elements related to story structure, such as mood or tone, could be used as well. Students then work in groups to create their Vocab-o-Grams, moving through the following steps:

1. Discuss the vocabulary words from the story.
2. Place the vocabulary words in the category on the graphic organizer where you think the author will use the words: setting, characters, conflict, plot, resolution.
3. Make predictions about the story using the vocabulary words to answer each of the questions in each of the story structure categories.
4. Students should list questions they have prior to reading the story. The vocabulary words, discussion, and elements of story structure will prompt students' questions.
5. Words which are too unfamiliar, or words which don't make sense in terms of students' questions and predictions, can be listed in the Mystery Words space on the graphic organizer.
6. After reading, students revisit their Vocab-o-Grams to answer the questions they wrote, define or describe context for mystery words, and revise predictions to reflect information from the story.
7. Vocab-o-Grams can then be used to scaffold writing about the story.

When and Why Would I Use a Vocab-o-Gram?

A Vocab-o-Gram is based on story structure (story grammar) and so could be used when you are using any narrative text. Given that this instructional activity is based on story structures, it would most often be used in an English or reading class although it could be used in any context where a story (narrative) text is being shared. Since the Vocab-o-Gram is both a prereading and a post-reading support for students, you would typically use this activity to build background knowledge, provide exposure to content-specific words, and generate predictions and questions related to a story prior to reading.

In the example shown here, Lynnette Elliott is using a Vocab-o-Gram for all these purposes prior to her high school students beginning their shared reading of *Lay That Trumpet in Our Hands* (McCarthy 2002). Students will use these words to predict the elements of the story, predict and question plot, and describe the connections between and among words in the word bank. Examples of students' predictions include the following:

- We think the author will use the words *citrus, paradise, grove,* and *processing plant* to describe the setting. Since the book takes place in Florida, the author might say, "The story takes place in a state which seems like paradise to Northerners. There are citrus groves near the processing plants, which make orange juice."
- We think there will be Crackers, Northerners, and Klansmen in the book. The Northerners might be seen as arrogant by Florida Crackers. And, the Klansmen are bigoted.
- We think the conflict will be between Klansmen and the Northerners. If there is a cross burning, it probably means the Klan will attack black people. Maybe the Northerners will stand up for the black people.
- We aren't sure what will happen but we think dynamite will be used to do something bad and there will be a warrant for someone's arrest.
- We think the story will end with someone's secret coming out.
- Our questions are:
  1. Is this a true story?
  2. Where in Florida does it take place?
  3. Who is prejudiced? Is it the Northerners or the Crackers or just the Klansmen?
- Words we don't know or can't use to make predictions: diamondbacks, snake-charmed, debatable, stranger, dialect, dominance.

VOCAB-O-GRAM
Lay That Trumpet in Our Hands

Use the vocabulary words in the word bank to make predictions about the book we are reading. You can use the words more than once to make your predictions. Think about how you think the author of the book will use the words in the story. List words that you think will go with each category of the story structure and then use those words to make predictions and answer the questions about structure. If there are words your group can't use because they are too unfamiliar, list those words at the bottom as Mystery Words.

Word Bank:				
	debatable	Northerners	prejudice	grove
snake-charmed	Crackers	uppity	bigoted	dominance
paradise	Klansmen	citrus	intolerance	diamondbacks
scandalous	arrogant	processing plant	warrant	cross-burning
secret	stranger	dialect	dynamite	

Setting How will the author describe the setting?	
Characters What predictions can you make about the characters?	
Conflict What will the conflict be? Who will be involved?	
Plot What will happen in the story?	
Resolution How will the story end?	
Questions What questions do you have about the story?	
Mystery Words	

Adapted from C. L. Z. Blachowicz (1986), "Making Connections: Alternatives to the Vocabulary Notebook," Journal of Reading 29: 643–49.

Students' Vocab-o-Grams can be revisited post-reading in order to help them review elements of story structure as well as the specific elements of the story you have read. Students' initial responses, predictions, and questions provide an ideal starting point for writing: story response or summary, character analysis, and essays about the author's craft or purpose.

Research/Origins/Further Reading

Blachowicz, C. L. Z. 1986. "Making Connections: Alternatives to the Vocabulary Notebook." *Journal of Reading* 29: 643–49.

Blachowicz, C., and P. J. Fisher. 2002. *Teaching Vocabulary in All Classrooms*. 2nd ed. Upper Saddle River, NJ: Pearson Education.

McCarthy, S. 2002. *Lay That Trumpet in Our Hands*. New York: Bantam Dell.

WORD SORT

What Is a Word Sort?

A Word Sort (Gillet and Temple 1983) is an activity where students are asked to sort words into categories by sorting words into groups where the words have a common element. The list of words that students sort is provided for them from a bank of words the teacher creates. Word Sorts can be open or closed. If students are provided with a word bank and asked to place words in categories you provide, that is a *closed* Word Sort. If students are given a word bank and asked to place words in categories they create, that is an *open* Word Sort. Unlike List-Group-Label (Taba 1967), words used in the Word Sort are provided by the teacher. In this way, the specific content vocabulary that will be or has been encountered in a unit of study can be discussed and connected to related words.

How Does It Work?

If a Word Sort is used as a prereading instructional strategy, you will create a bank of words related to the unit of study. In the example shown here, the teacher has created an *open* Word Sort for students. Prior to reading the chapter "The Rise of Rome" in their World History textbook, students will work in groups to discuss the vocabulary words from the text's chapter. The teacher has created a word bank which students will use in their discussion. After discussing the words, students will group them by determining words which have something in common. Students should be able to justify their categories and the words they have placed in the categories. One category created by most groups in the class was labeled, "Government." Those groups creating this category of words, placed the following words in the category: senate, judicial, branch, legislative, executive.

If this World History teacher had wanted to create a closed Word Sort, he would have provided students with the categories. A closed Word Sort for this study could have included the following categories: government, socioeconomic structures, political power/politicians, legacy, and society. Students would work in groups to sort words in the word bank into the categories provided by the teacher.

When Would I Use a Word Sort?

Word Sorts can be used as prereading where students would encounter the content-specific words about to be studied or it can be used as a post-reading review and assessment of students' knowledge of related content. A Word Sort done prior to students' reading a text will provide you with an initial assessment of students' background knowledge of the words and concepts they will encounter when reading the text. When students are justifying their categories, it

WORD SORT
The Rise of Rome

Examine and discuss the words listed below. Group the words into categories so the words in each category share common elements. Your group should be able to explain your categories and justify your reasons for including the words in each category.

emperor	Rome	branch	citizenship
gladiators	rivalry	senate	form
ambition	executive	plebeians	social class
republic	patricians	balances	
overthrow	judicial	assassinated	
tripartite	Julius Caesar	toga	
Colosseum	checks	legislative	

provides you with an opportunity to lead and guide the discussion so basic information related to the words is recorded.

Research/Origins/Further Reading

Allen, J. 2004. *Tools for Teaching Content Literacy*. Portland, ME: Stenhouse.

Billmeyer, R. 2003. *Strategies to Engage the Mind of the Learner.*
Omaha, NE: Dayspring.

———. 2004. *Strategic Reading in the Content Areas: Practical
Applications for Creating a Thinking Environment.* Omaha, NE:
Dayspring.

Ganske, K. 2006. *Word Sorts and More: Sound, Pattern, and
Meaning Explorations K–3.* New York: Guilford Press.

Gillet, J. W., and C. Temple. 1986. *Understanding Reading Problems:
Assessment and Instruction.* 2nd ed. Boston: Little, Brown.

Taba, H. 1967. *Teacher's Handbook for Elementary Social Studies.*
Reading, MA: Addison-Wesley.

WORD WALLS

What Is a Word Wall?

A Word Wall (Cunningham and Allington 1994) is a displayed collection of words that support ongoing teaching and learning in the classroom. Words collected on the Word Wall could be *high-utility words*. These are words that are used often in an individual classroom. A *high-utility* Word Wall in a math class would consist of math terms used throughout the year. A *topical* Word Wall consists of words related to a theme, text, or unit of instruction; for example, the Revolutionary War.

How Do Word Walls Work?

Word Walls can work in a variety of ways to support reading, writing, and talk in your classroom. If you are creating and using a *high-utility* Word Wall, you will want to add words to the Word Wall as they are encountered in the course of students' learning. These words should be added as encountered in shared reading and study of individual words. The words should be ones you would want students to use in their writing and conversation.

If you are creating and using a *topical* Word Wall, the wall will contain words supporting your current concept/thematic study, unit of instruction, or extended text. Two different examples are shown here. In the first example, students are collecting those frequently used words they have discovered when reading works by Shakespeare. On this Word Wall, students are recording the Shakespearean word or phrase and its meaning. In the second example, students are collecting words during their reading of *The Last Book in the Universe* (Philbrick 2002). Because this book is science fiction, language is a critical issue in terms of comprehension and the writing students will do related to the text. Students are collecting words that are new to them as well as familiar words that have a new use in the context of this novel. Because the book is science fiction, there is a large amount of scientific, environmental, and futuristic language so students are gathering those words as well. Finally, students are collecting terms that are slang for those living in this futuristic society.

When and Why Would I Use a Word Wall?

Word Walls can make an immediate and significant difference in students' academic writing. I have found few Word Walls that are successful if they are prepared in the absence of teaching and learning. You will want your Word Wall to be a living part of the classroom with new words being added each day as they are encountered and taught. Words on the wall should be spelled correctly so students have access to

SIGHT WORDS FOR SHAKESPEARE

A–B	C–D	E–F
		fortnight—two weeks

G–H	I–J	K–L
go to-stop—that's enough		**let's away**—let's go

M–N	O–P	Q–R
		rest you merry—good-bye/stay happy **rapier**—sword

S–T	U–V	WXYZ
soft—wait a minute **sirrah**—term used to address servants **stinted**—cried	**visor**—mask	**what**—where are you?

Example 1

them during academic writing. As a way to support students' homework and writing in and outside class, students can keep a portable Word Wall in their academic notebooks. Students receive a new Portable Word Wall form for each new unit of study. They label the topic of the Word Wall; collect related words they encounter; and make notes at the bottom about word meanings as well as connections between and among words. In a classroom I recently visited, students were collecting words related to digestion and used the word notes space to draw a diagram with labels in order to help them remember related words.

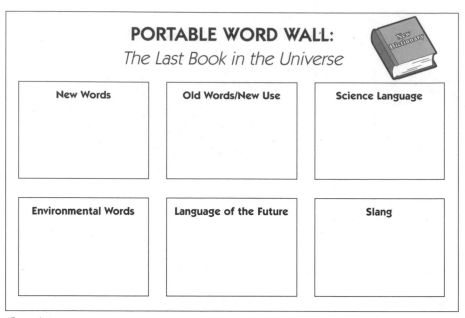

PORTABLE WORD WALL:
The Last Book in the Universe

New Words	Old Words/New Use	Science Language

Environmental Words	Language of the Future	Slang

Example 2

Research/Origins/Further Reading

Cunningham, P. M., and R. L. Allington. 1994. *Classrooms That Work: They Can All Read and Write*. New York: HarperCollins College.

Philbrick, R. 2002. *The Last Book in the Universe*. New York: Blue Sky Press/Scholastic.

APPENDIX

CONCEPT CIRCLES

Look at the items in the concept circle. Write about your understanding of _____ by highlighting the connections between and among each of the items in the concept circle. What is the significance of each one and how do the items in the concept circle fit together?

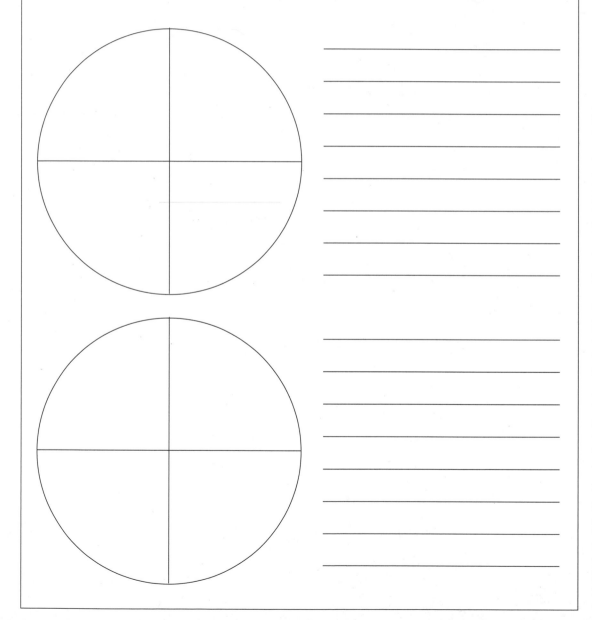

CÍRCULOS CONCEPTUALES

Observa los artículos en el círculo conceptual. Escribe acerca de tu comprensión de _____ resaltando las conexiones entre cada uno de los artículos, uno con otro y el total, en el círculo conceptual. ¿Qué importancia tiene cada uno y cómo se adecuan entre sí los artículos?

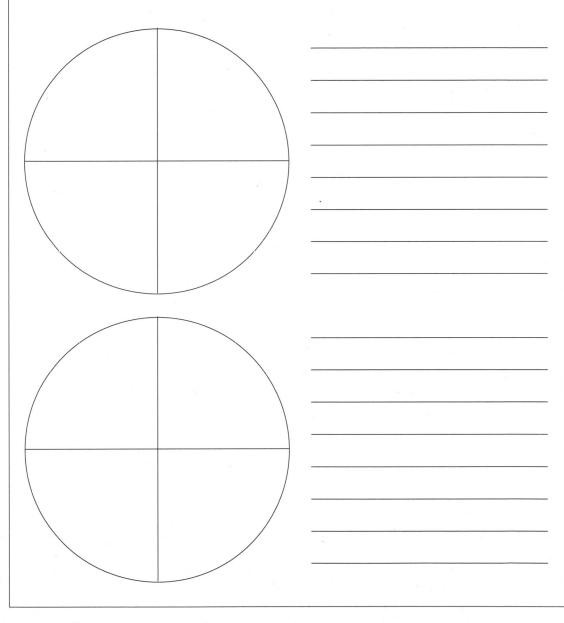

CONCEPT LADDER

Concept:

Adapted from J. W. Gillet and C. Temple (1986)

Inside Words: Tools for Teaching Academic Vocabulary, Grades 4–12 by Janet Allen. Copyright © 2007. Stenhouse Publishers.

ESCALERA CONCEPTUAL

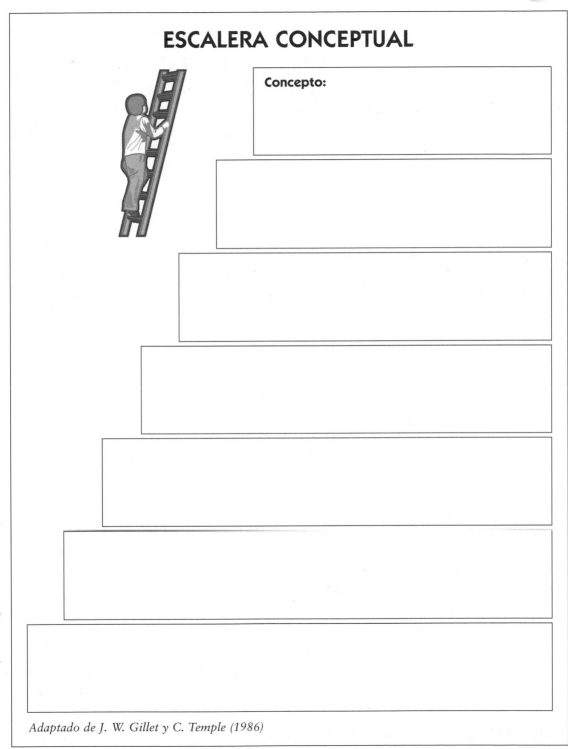

Concepto:

Adaptado de J. W. Gillet y C. Temple (1986)

CONCEPTS AND VOCABULARY: CATEGORIES AND LABELS

Read and think about each of the words you have been given. Now, group the words into categories that make logical sense to you. Ask yourself which words would logically go together. After you group the words, give each group a label. Be ready to explain or justify the rationale behind your groups and labels.

Words:

Inside Words: Tools for Teaching Academic Vocabulary, Grades 4–12 by Janet Allen. Copyright © 2007. Stenhouse Publishers.

CONCEPTOS Y VOCABULARIO: CATEGORÍAS Y RÓTULOS

Lee y reflexiona acerca de cada una de las palabras que tienes. Ahora, agrupa las palabras en categorías que tengan una lógica para ti. Piensa qué palabras irían juntas, si siguen una lógica. Después de agrupar las palabras, rotula cada grupo. Trata de tener listos tus argumentos para explicar o justificar el razonamiento que usas para hacer tus grupos y rótulos.

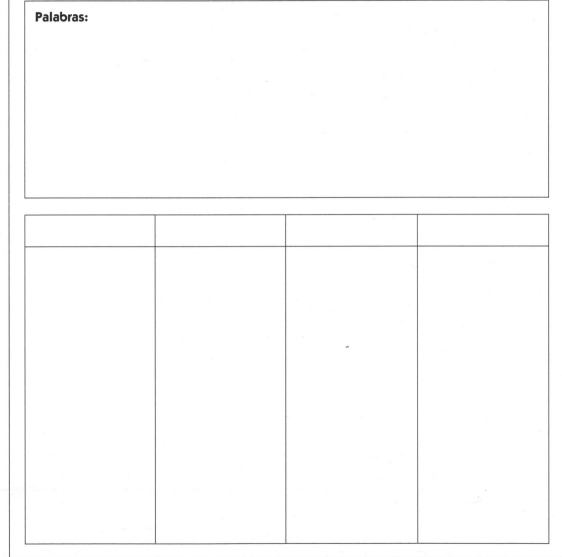

Palabras:

CONTEXTUAL REDEFINITION

Work with a group to make predictions for definitions of each of the following words. The words included here are found in _____. Remember that some words which look familiar will probably have new meanings in this context.

Word	Predicted Definition	Definition Based on Context	Context Clues Used

Based on this activity, I've learned the following strategies for determining word meaning through context clues:

REDEFINICIÓN CONTEXTUAL

Inside Words: Tools for Teaching Academic Vocabulary, Grades 4–12 by Janet Allen. Copyright © 2007. Stenhouse Publishers.

Trabaja en grupo y trata de hacer predicciones para las definiciones de cada una de las siguientes palabras. Las palabras aquí incluidas se encuentran en _____. Recuerda que algunas palabras que suenan conocidas probablemente tengan nuevos significados en este contexto.

Palabra	Definición predicha	Definición basada en el contexto	Pistas del contexto que se usaron

Basándome en esta actividad, he aprendido las siguientes estrategias para determinar el significado de palabras a través de pistas en el contexto:

DICTOGLOS

Words/Phrases	Group Words/Phrases
Group Version of Text	**Compare to Original Text**

Inside Words: Tools for Teaching Academic Vocabulary, Grades 4–12 by Janet Allen. Copyright © 2007. Stenhouse Publishers.

DICTOGLOS

Palabras/Frases	Palabras grupales/Frases
Versión grupal del texto	**Comparar con el texto original**

FRAYER MODEL

Define the concept	Is different from similar concepts . . .
Examples of the concept are . . .	**Nonexamples of the concept are . . .**

I'll remember the word by . . .

Inside Words: Tools for Teaching Academic Vocabulary, Grades 4–12 by Janet Allen. Copyright © 2007. Stenhouse Publishers.

MODELO DE FRAYER

Define el concepto	Es diferente de otros conceptos similares . . .
Son ejemplos del concepto . . .	**No son ejemplos del concepto . . .**

Recordaré la palabra mediante . . .

Inside Words: Tools for Teaching Academic Vocabulary, Grades 4–12 by Janet Allen. Copyright © 2007. Stenhouse Publishers.

FREQUENT CONTACT

Read and discuss each of the words in the word bank. As you discuss the words, decide which column each should be placed in based on which words would have the most frequent contact with each category's label. If you can justify placing words in more than one category, you should do that. When you finish, circle those words that ended up in more than one category.

Adapted from S. Jantzen. 1985. Scholastic Composition, *Level 2. New York: Scholastic.*

Inside Words: Tools for Teaching Academic Vocabulary, Grades 4–12 by Janet Allen. Copyright © 2007. Stenhouse Publishers.

CONTACTO FRECUENTE

Lee y comenta cada una de las palabras del banco de palabras. A medida que comentas las palabras, decide en qué columna debe ir cada una basándote en qué palabras tendrían el contacto más frecuente con el rótulo de cada categoría. Si puedes justificar colocar palabras en más de una categoría, debes hacerlo. Cuando termines, rodea con un círculo las palabras que quedan ubicadas en más de una categoría.

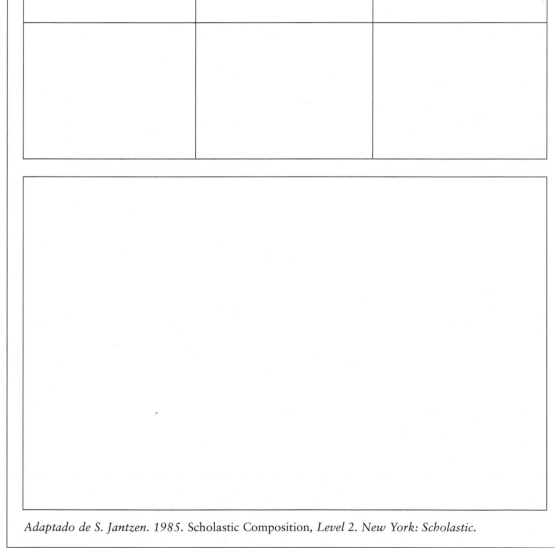

Adaptado de S. Jantzen. 1985. Scholastic Composition, *Level 2. New York: Scholastic.*

Inside Words: Tools for Teaching Academic Vocabulary, Grades 4–12 by Janet Allen. Copyright © 2007. Stenhouse Publishers.

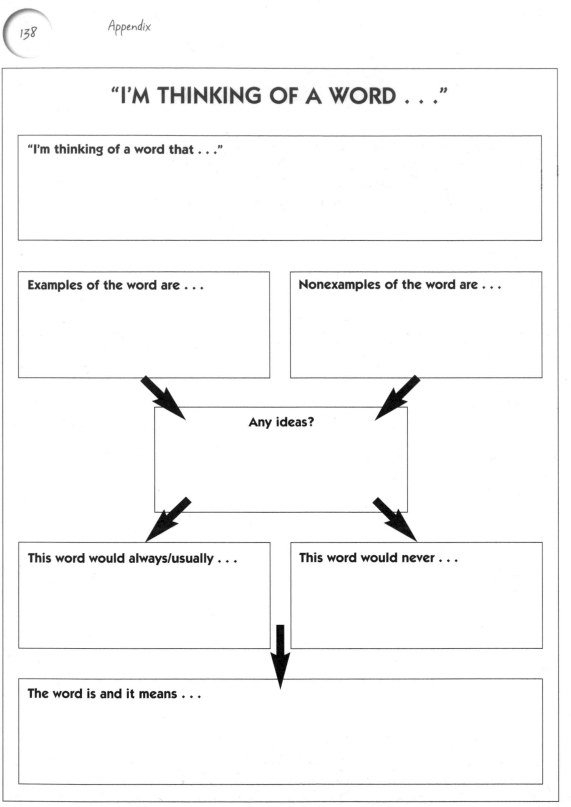

"I'M THINKING OF A WORD . . ."

"I'm thinking of a word that . . ."

Examples of the word are . . .

Nonexamples of the word are . . .

Any ideas?

This word would always/usually . . .

This word would never . . .

The word is and it means . . .

Inside Words: Tools for Teaching Academic Vocabulary, Grades 4–12 by Janet Allen. Copyright © 2007. Stenhouse Publishers.

"PIENSO EN UNA PALABRA QUE . . ."

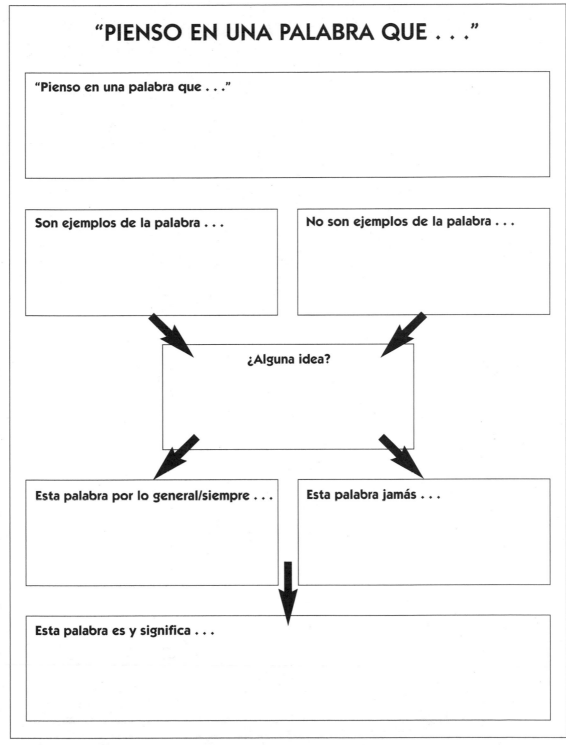

"Pienso en una palabra que . . ."

Son ejemplos de la palabra . . .

No son ejemplos de la palabra . . .

¿Alguna idea?

Esta palabra por lo general/siempre . . .

Esta palabra jamás . . .

Esta palabra es y significa . . .

I SPY: A WORD SCAVENGER HUNT

Word/Concept	Where Discovered?	Word Artifact	Definition/ Connection to Unit of Study

Inside Words: Tools for Teaching Academic Vocabulary, Grades 4–12 by Janet Allen. Copyright © 2007. Stenhouse Publishers.

YO ESPÍO: CAZA DE PALABRAS

Palabra/Concepto	¿Dónde se descubrió?	Artefacto de la palabra	Definición/ Conexión con la unidad de estudio

LEAD
EXPERIENCE-BASED VOCABULARY INSTRUCTION

L = Listing   EA = Experience Activity   D = Discussion

List

Experience Activity

Discussion

Adapted from J. P. Klesius and S. E. Klesius (1989) and from J. M. Jacobson (1998)

Inside Words: Tools for Teaching Academic Vocabulary, Grades 4–12 by Janet Allen. Copyright © 2007. Stenhouse Publishers.

LEAD
INSTRUCCIÓN DE VOCABULARIO CON BASE EN LA EXPERIENCIA

L = Listado   EA = Experiencia Actividad   D = Discusión

Listado

Experiencia Actividad

Discusión

Adaptado de J. P. Klesius y S. E. Klesius (1989) y de J. M. Jacobson (1998)

LIST-GROUP-LABEL

My brainstorming list for _____

Word patterns our group discovered . . .

Based on our words and labels, we can make the following statements about this topic:

Inside Words: Tools for Teaching Academic Vocabulary, Grades 4–12 by Janet Allen. Copyright © 2007. Stenhouse Publishers.

LISTAR-CATEGORIZAR-ROTULAR

Mi lista de la lluvia de ideas para _____

Patrones de palabras que descubrió nuestro grupo . . .

Basándonos en nuestras palabras y rótulos, podemos hacer las siguientes oraciones acerca de este tema:

POSSIBLE QUESTIONS

Possible Questions That
Will Be Answered

1. [ ] + [ ] + [ ] = _____

2. [ ] + [ ] + [ ] = _____

3. [ ] + [ ] + [ ] = _____

4. [ ] + [ ] + [ ] = _____

5. [ ] + [ ] + [ ] = _____

Checking Understanding

Answer to my question or new question and answer:

1.

2.

3.

4.

5.

Create a visual representation (with labels) that shows what you have learned.

Inside Words: Tools for Teaching Academic Vocabulary, Grades 4–12 by Janet Allen. Copyright © 2007. Stenhouse Publishers.

Inside Words: Tools for Teaching Academic Vocabulary, Grades 4–12 by Janet Allen. Copyright © 2007. Stenhouse Publishers.

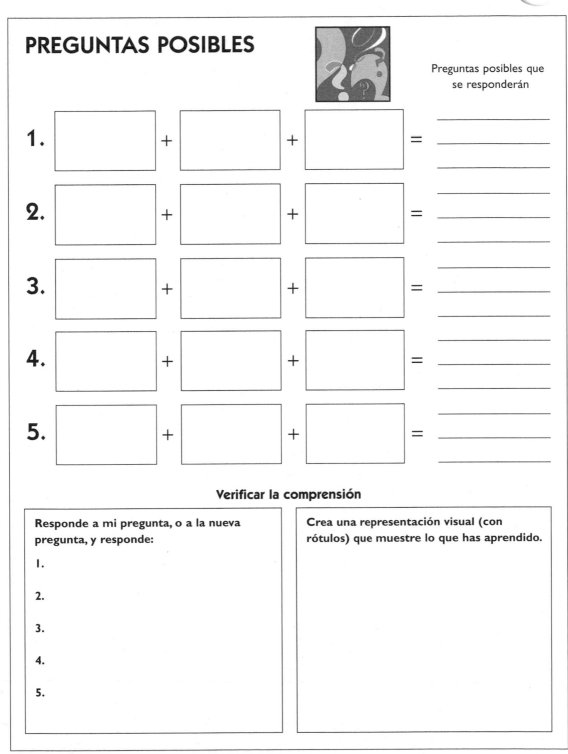

PREGUNTAS POSIBLES

Preguntas posibles que
se responderán

1. [ ] + [ ] + [ ] = _____

2. [ ] + [ ] + [ ] = _____

3. [ ] + [ ] + [ ] = _____

4. [ ] + [ ] + [ ] = _____

5. [ ] + [ ] + [ ] = _____

Verificar la comprensión

**Responde a mi pregunta, o a la nueva
pregunta, y responde:**

1.

2.

3.

4.

5.

**Crea una representación visual (con
rótulos) que muestre lo que has aprendido.**

POSSIBLE SENTENCES

Possible Sentences

1.
2.
3.
4.
5.
6.
7.
8.
9.
10.

Using Sentences as a Guide/Modifying Predictions

Mark each of the possible sentences with True, False, or Unknown. When you finish reading, return to your sentences and see how you could modify them so they are accurate in terms of the content of the passage you have read.

1.
2.
3.
4.
5.
6.
7.
8.
9.
10.

Inside Words: Tools for Teaching Academic Vocabulary, Grades 4–12 by Janet Allen. Copyright © 2007. Stenhouse Publishers.

ORACIONES POSIBLES

Inside Words: Tools for Teaching Academic Vocabulary, Grades 4–12 by Janet Allen. Copyright © 2007. Stenhouse Publishers.

Oraciones posibles

1.

2.

3.

4.

5.

6.

7.

8.

9.

10.

Uso de oraciones como guía o para modificar predicciones

Marca cada una de las oraciones posibles con Verdadero, Falso o Desconocido. Cuando termines de leer, vuelve a las oraciones y piensa cómo podrías modificarlas para que sean exactas en términos del contenido del pasaje que has leído.

1.

2.

3.

4.

5.

6.

7.

8.

9.

10.

PREVIEWING CONTENT VOCABULARY

Based on the title, words I would expect to read in this chapter:

I've never heard the word . . .	I've heard the word, but I don't know what it means . . .
I think the word means or is related to . . .	**I know the word . . .**

Content Vocabulary

Inside Words: Tools for Teaching Academic Vocabulary. Grades 4–12 by Janet Allen. Copyright © 2007. Stenhouse Publishers.

Inside Words: Tools for Teaching Academic Vocabulary, Grades 4–12 by Janet Allen. Copyright © 2007. Stenhouse Publishers.

PREVISUALIZAR EL VOCABULARIO DEL CONTENIDO

Según el título, estas son palabras que yo esperaría leer en este capítulo:

Nunca he oído la palabra . . .	**He oído la palabra, pero no sé lo que significa . . .**
Pienso que la palabra significa o está relacionada con . . .	**Conozco la palabra . . .**

Vocabulario del contenido

SEMANTIC FEATURE ANALYSIS

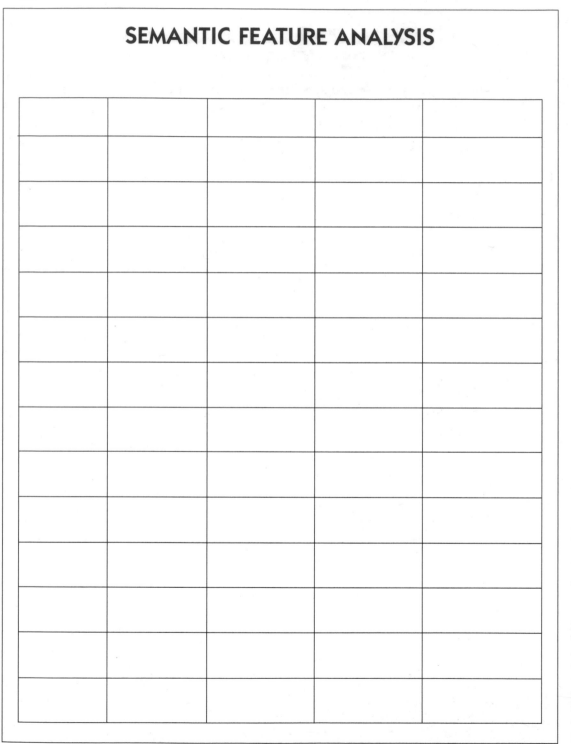

Inside Words: Tools for Teaching Academic Vocabulary, Grades 4–12 by Janet Allen. Copyright © 2007. Stenhouse Publishers.

ANÁLISIS DE CARACTERÍSTICAS SEMÁNTICAS

SURVIVAL OF THE FITTEST

Read and discuss the words in each of the clusters of words. Determine which word does not fit with the other words in each cluster. Eliminate that word and then create a label that would include the words that are left in the cluster of words. For a challenge, generate a new word that would replace the eliminated word *and* fit with the remaining words in the cluster.

1. _____

2. _____

3. _____

4. _____

5. _____

6. _____

7. _____

8. _____

9. _____

10. _____

Inside Words: Tools for Teaching Academic Vocabulary, Grades 4–12 by Janet Allen. Copyright © 2007. Stenhouse Publishers.

SOBREVIVE LA QUE MEJOR SE ADAPTA

Lee y discute las palabras en cada uno de los grupos de palabras. Determina qué palabra no va con las otras en cada grupo. Elimina la palabra y luego crea un rótulo que pueda abarcar las palabras que quedan en el grupo de palabras. Como reto, genera una palabra nueva que reemplace la palabra eliminada y vaya con las restantes palabras en el grupo.

1. _____

2. _____

3. _____

4. _____

5. _____

6. _____

7. _____

8. _____

9. _____

10. _____

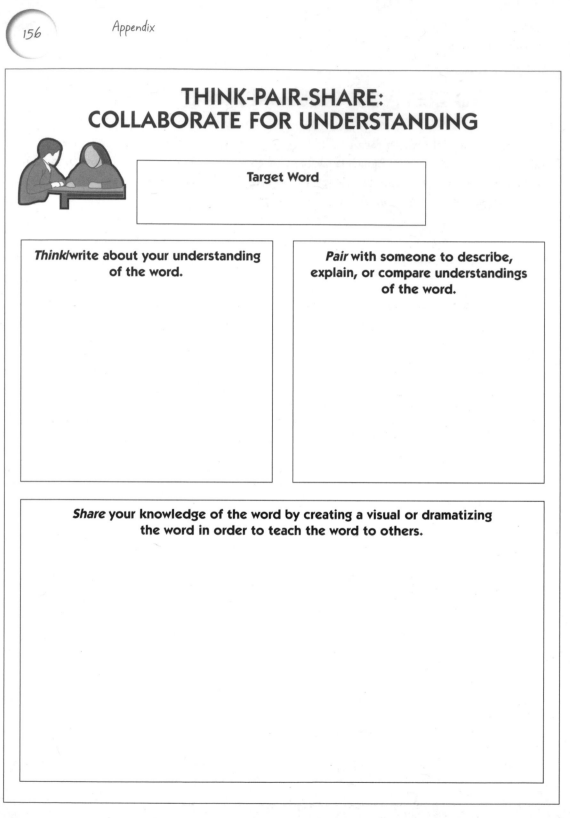

THINK-PAIR-SHARE:
COLLABORATE FOR UNDERSTANDING

Target Word

Think/write about your understanding of the word.

Pair with someone to describe, explain, or compare understandings of the word.

Share your knowledge of the word by creating a visual or dramatizing the word in order to teach the word to others.

PENSAR-UNIRSE-COMPARTIR: COLABORAR PARA LA COMPRENSIÓN

Palabra objetivo

Piensa/escribe acerca de tu comprensión de la palabra.

Únete con un compañero para describir, explicar o comparar las comprensiones de la palabra.

Comparte tu conocimiento de la palabra mediante la creación de una ayuda visual o la dramatización de la palabra, para así enseñar la palabra a otros.

VOCAB-O-GRAM

Use the vocabulary words in the word bank to make predictions about the book we are reading. You can use the words more than once to make your predictions. Think about how you think the author of the book will use the words in the story. List words that you think will go with each category of the story structure and then use those words to make predictions and answer the questions about structure. If there are words your group can't use because they are too unfamiliar, list those words at the bottom as Mystery Words.

Word Bank:

Setting How will the author describe the setting?	
Characters What predictions can you make about the characters?	
Conflict What will the conflict be? Who will be involved?	
Plot What will happen in the story?	
Resolution How will the story end?	
Questions What questions do you have about the story?	
Mystery Words	

Inside Words: Tools for Teaching Academic Vocabulary, Grades 4–12 by Janet Allen. Copyright © 2007. Stenhouse Publishers.

Inside Words: Tools for Teaching Academic Vocabulary, Grades 4–12 by Janet Allen. Copyright © 2007. Stenhouse Publishers.

VOCAB-O-GRAM

Usa las palabras de vocabulario en el banco de palabras para hacer predicciones acerca del libro que estamos leyendo. Puedes usar las palabras más de una vez para hacer tus predicciones. Piensa cómo el autor del libro, según tu criterio, usará las palabras en el cuento. Haz una lista de las palabras que, según tu criterio, van con cada categoría de la estructura del cuento y luego usa esas palabras para hacer predicciones y responder las preguntas acerca de estructura. Si hay palabras que tu grupo no pueda usar porque suenan demasiado desconocidas, haz una lista de esas palabras al pie de la página, con el título de Palabras misteriosas.

Banco de palabras:

Escenario ¿Cómo el autor describirá el escenario?	
Personajes ¿Qué predicciones puedes hacer acerca de los personajes?	
Conflicto ¿Qué conflicto habrá? ¿Quién estará involucrado?	
Trama ¿Qué ocurrirá en el cuento?	
Desenlace ¿Cómo terminará el cuento?	
Preguntas ¿Qué preguntas tienes acerca del cuento?	
Palabras misteriosas	

WORD SORT

Examine and discuss the words listed below. Group the words into categories so the words in each category share common elements. Your group should be able to explain your categories and justify your reasons for including the words in each category.

Inside Words: Tools for Teaching Academic Vocabulary, Grades 4–12 by Janet Allen. Copyright © 2007. Stenhouse Publishers.

CLASIFICACIÓN DE PALABRAS

Examina y comenta las palabras de la lista más abajo. Agrupa las palabras en categorías para que las palabras en cada categoría compartan elementos comunes. Tu grupo debería ser capaz de explicar las categorías y justificar las razones para incluir las palabras en cada categoría.

PORTABLE WORD WALL

A–B	C–D	E–F

G–H	I–J	K–L

M–N	O–P	Q–R

S–T	U–V	WXYZ

Word Notes:

Inside Words: Tools for Teaching Academic Vocabulary, Grades 4–12 by Janet Allen. Copyright © 2007. Stenhouse Publishers.

AFICHE PORTÁTIL DE PALABRAS

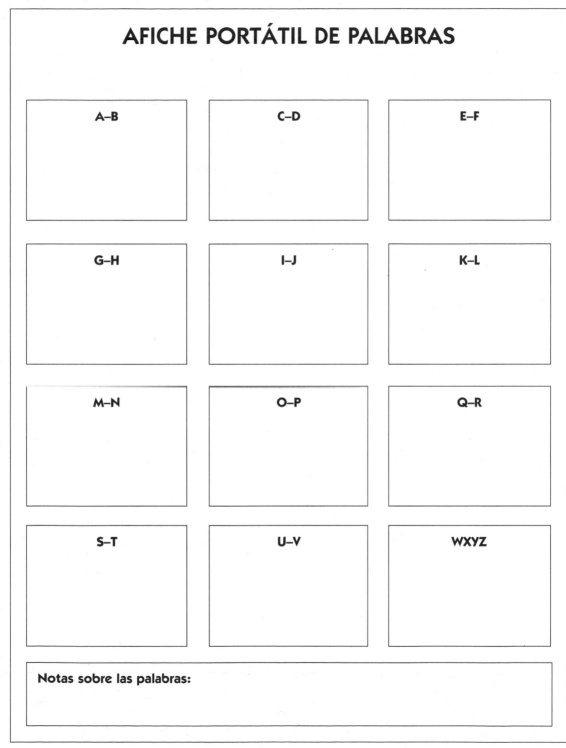

A–B	C–D	E–F
G–H	I–J	K–L
M–N	O–P	Q–R
S–T	U–V	WXYZ

Notas sobre las palabras: